Colour The Inner World

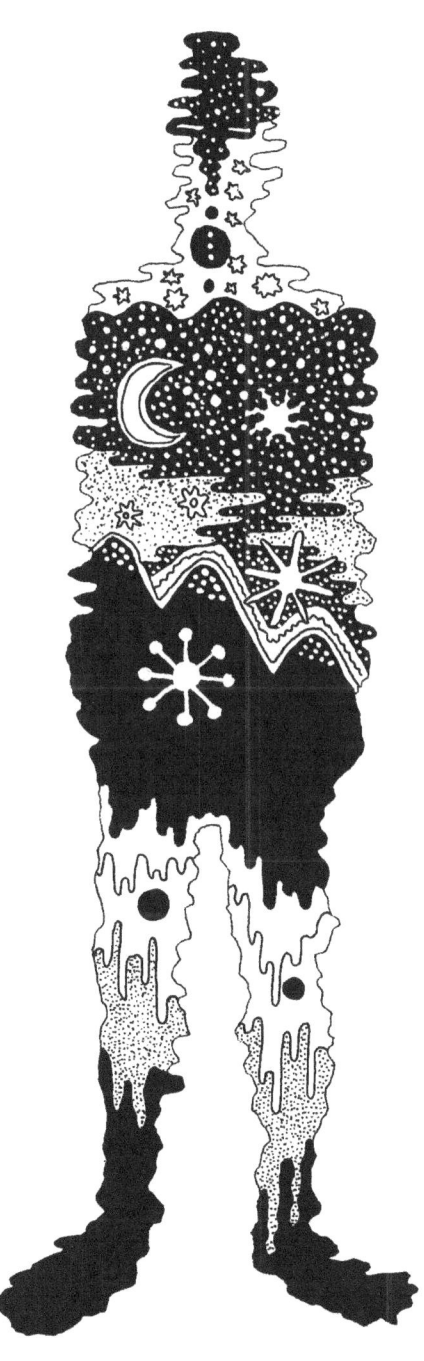

Daniel Arce

About the Author

Daniel Arce (DJ chile) is a scratch DJ, music educator, and artist from Hull, England. Daniel has a first class bachelor of arts degree in Creative Music Technology from the University of Hull. Daniel's art is heavily influenced by Psychology, Philosophy, Buddhism and often adopts a note taking style, mixing writing with drawings in an attempt to break down topics into visual analogies for self learning purposes.

 Instagram.com/dj.chile

 facebook.com/danielarceart

 Official site - *Ambivalentworks.com*

Other works by Daniel Arce -

Knowable knowns; Unknowable Unknowns is a creative attempt to merge multiple disparate threads of knowledge together in a sometimes cohesive, sometimes shrouded and thought provoking format. A sprawling mesh of illustrations and writings whose purpose is to point the reader in various often contradictory directions in an attempt to challenge and provoke self contemplation.

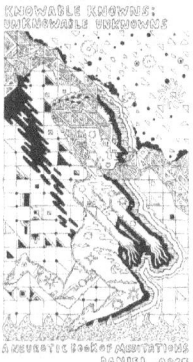

Contents

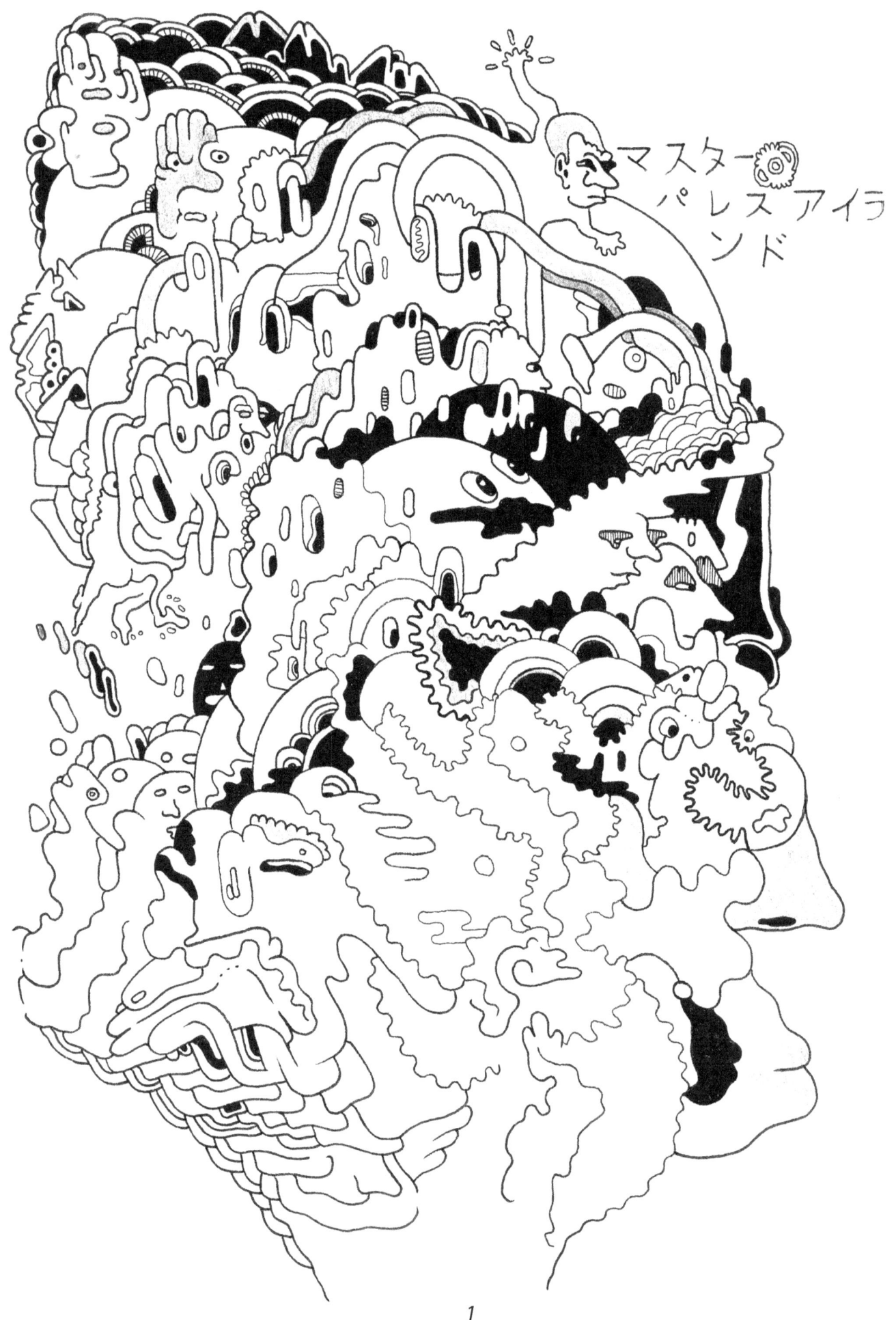

マスター
パレス アイラ
ンド

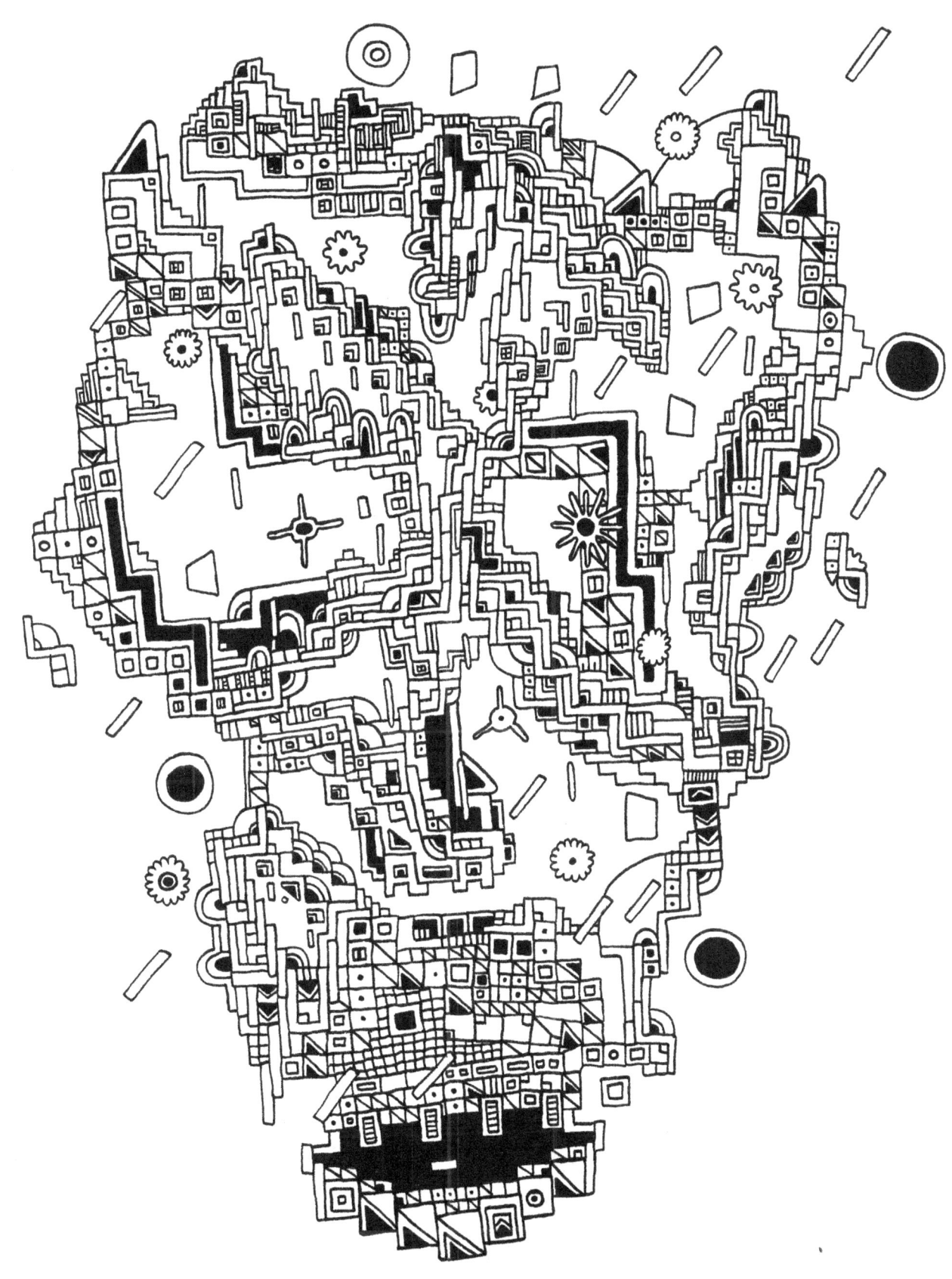

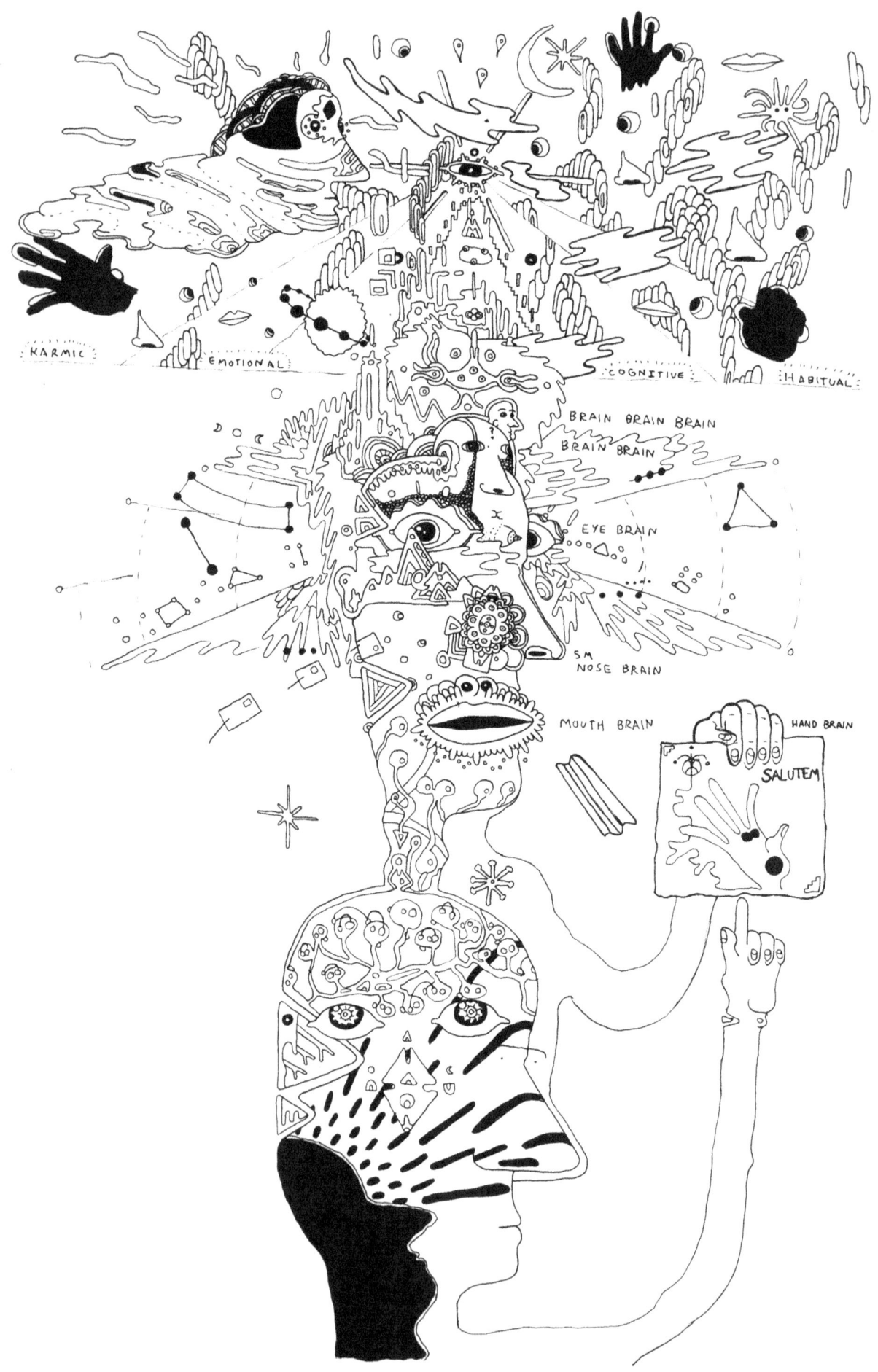

KARMIC   EMOTIONAL   COGNITIVE   HABITUAL

BRAIN BRAIN BRAIN
BRAIN BRAIN

EYE BRAIN

SM
NOSE BRAIN

MOUTH BRAIN   HAND BRAIN

SALUTEM

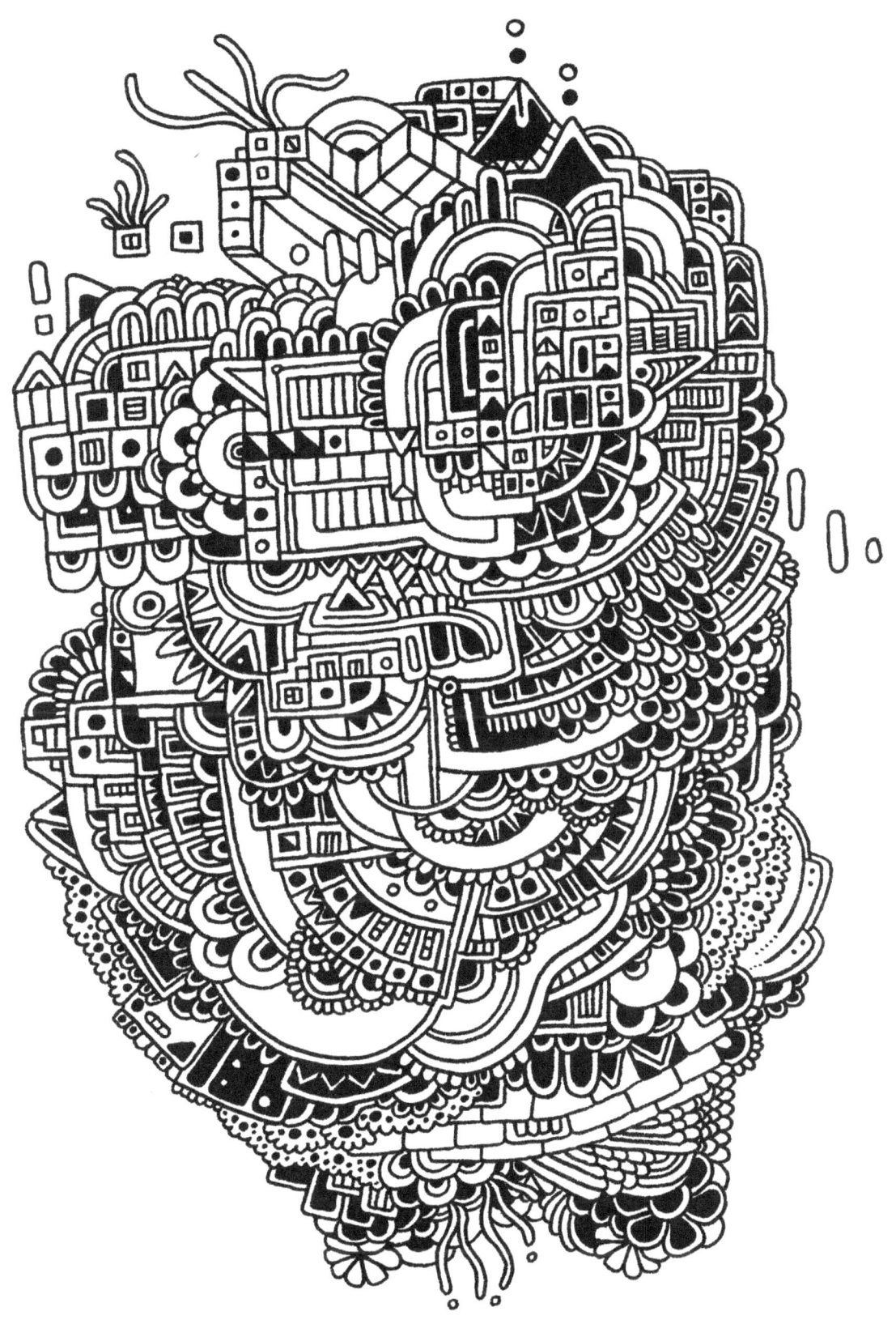

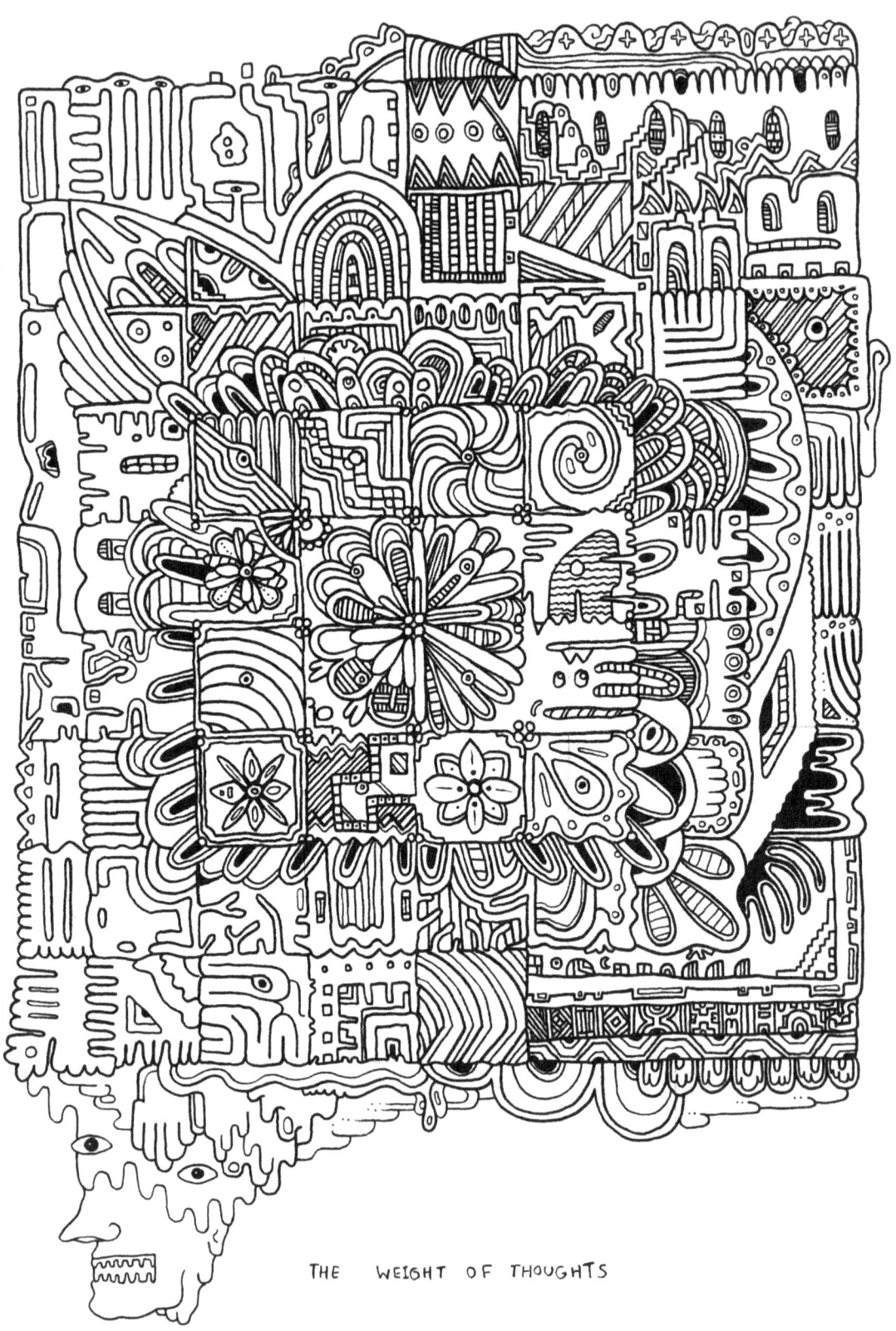

THE WEIGHT OF THOUGHTS

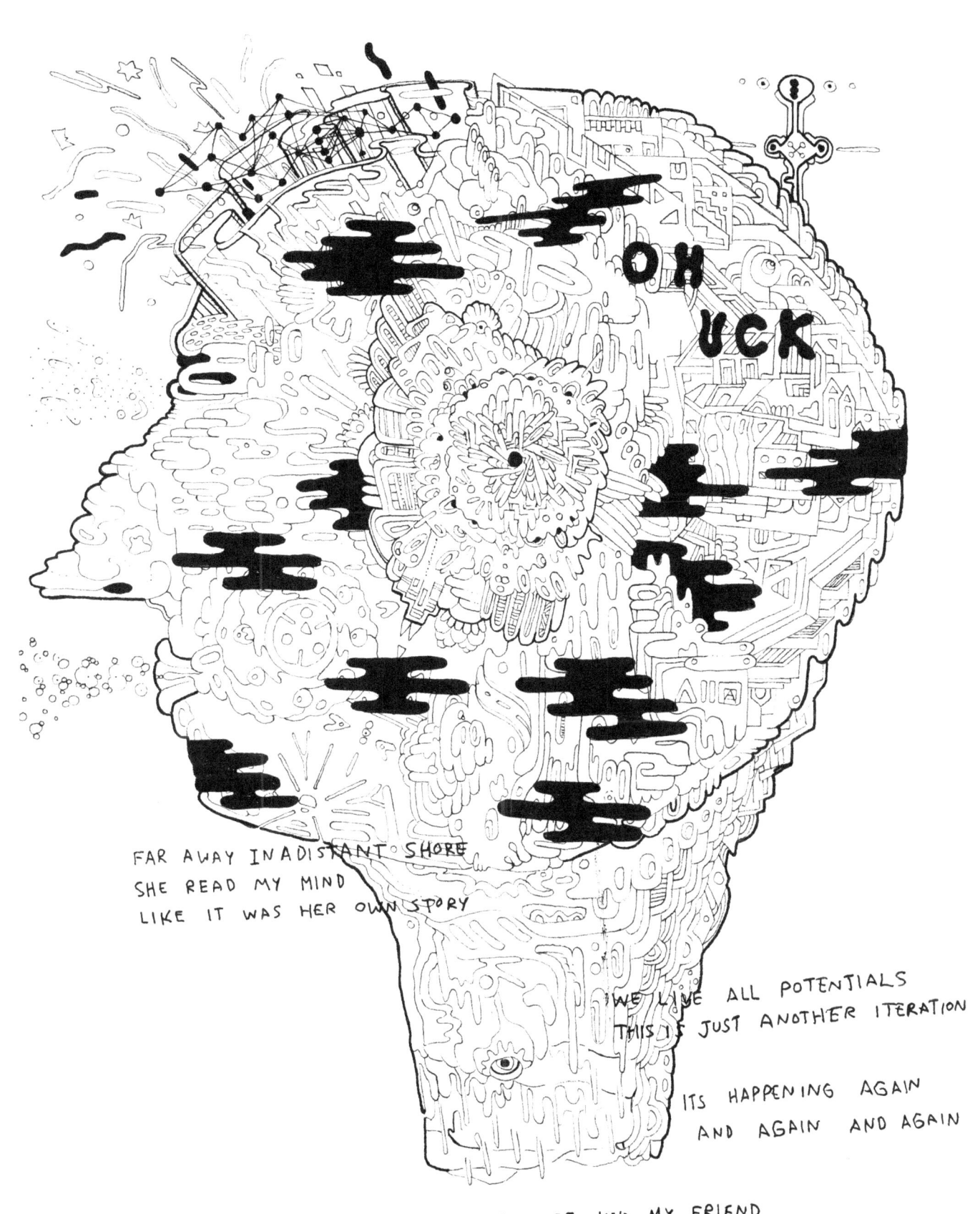

FAR AWAY IN A DISTANT SHORE
SHE READ MY MIND
LIKE IT WAS HER OWN STORY

WE LIVE ALL POTENTIALS
THIS IS JUST ANOTHER ITERATION

ITS HAPPENING AGAIN
AND AGAIN AND AGAIN

AND WHERE ARE YOU MY FRIEND
MY FRIEND FROM YESTERDAY
MY FRIEND FROM TOMMOROW

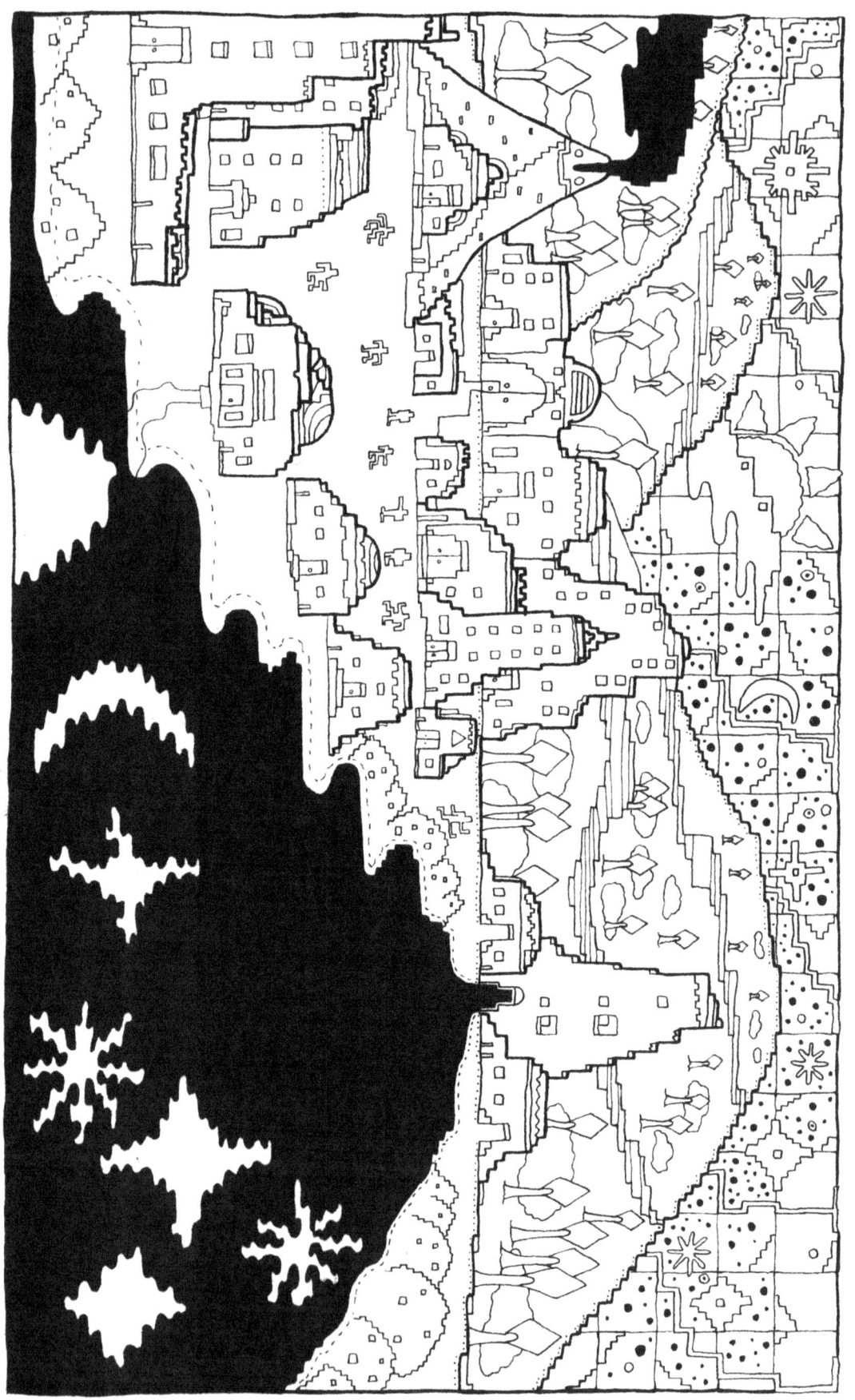

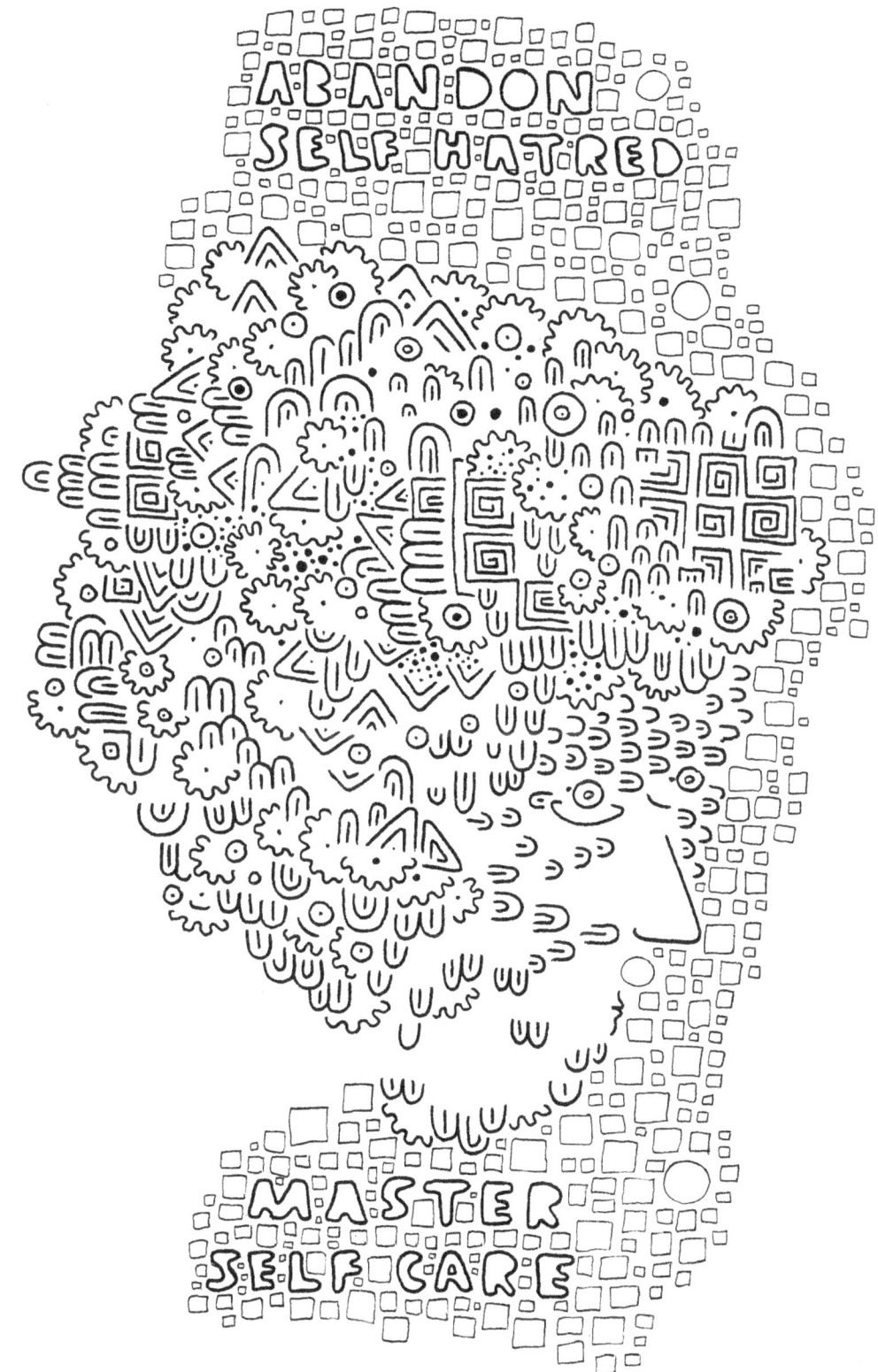

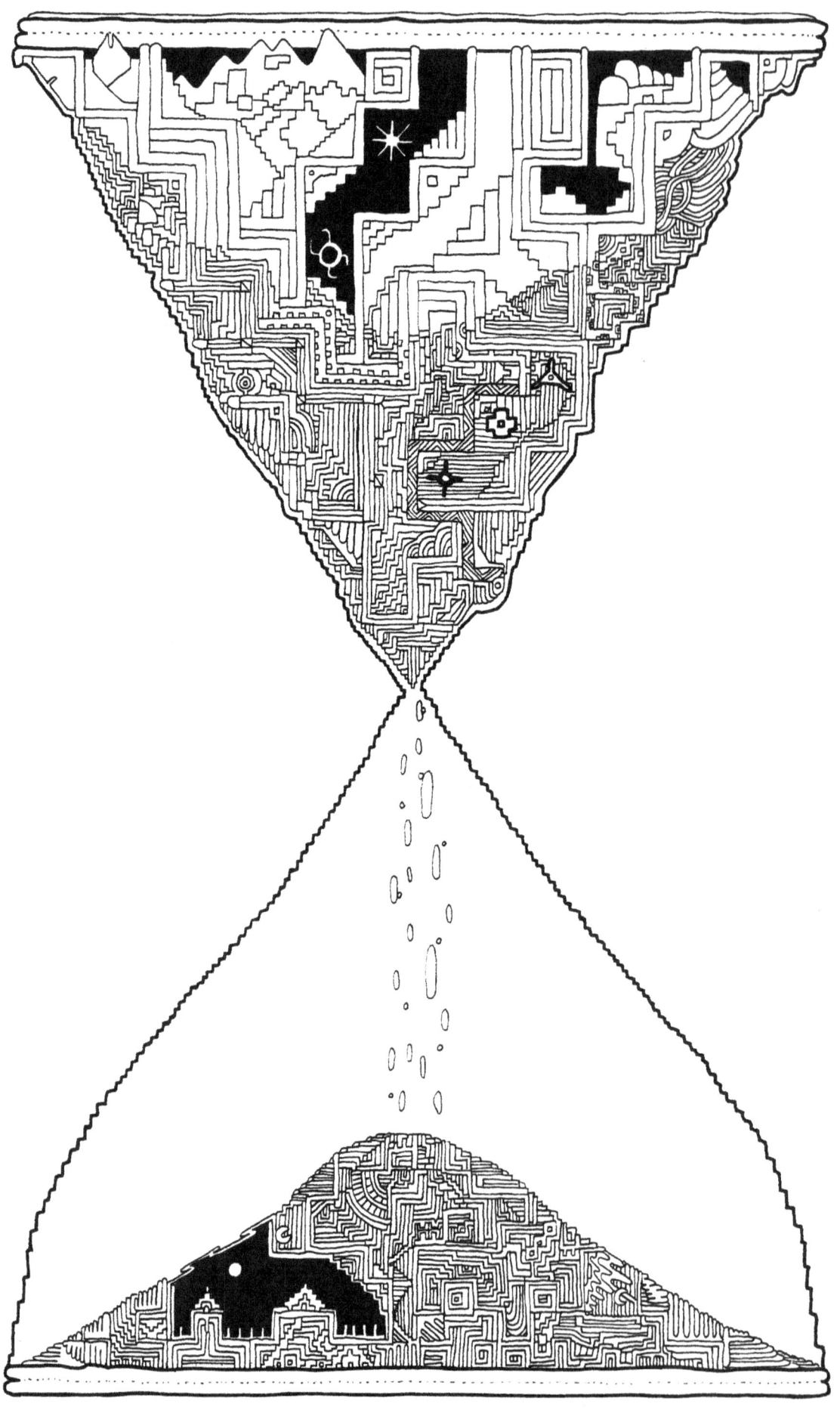

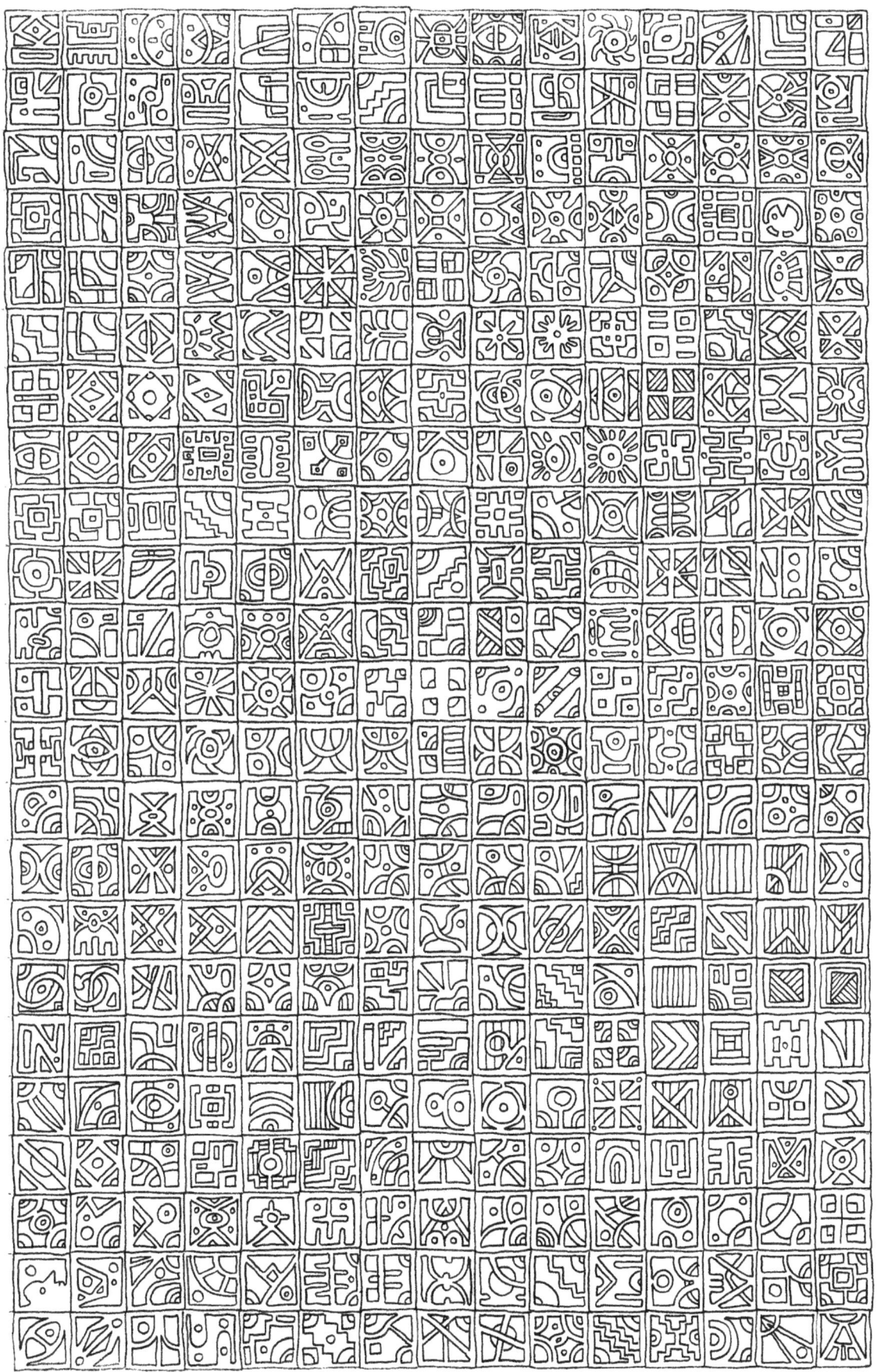

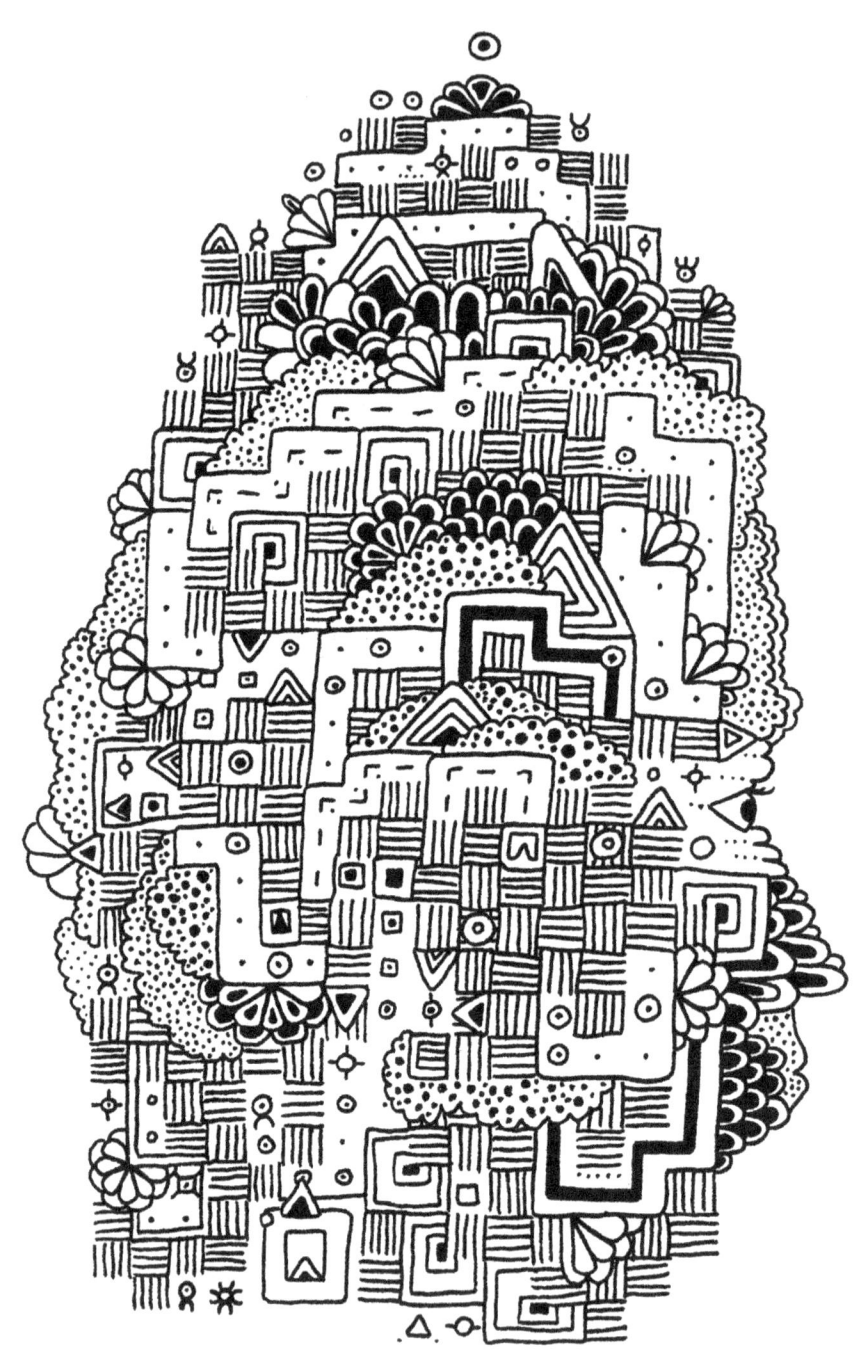

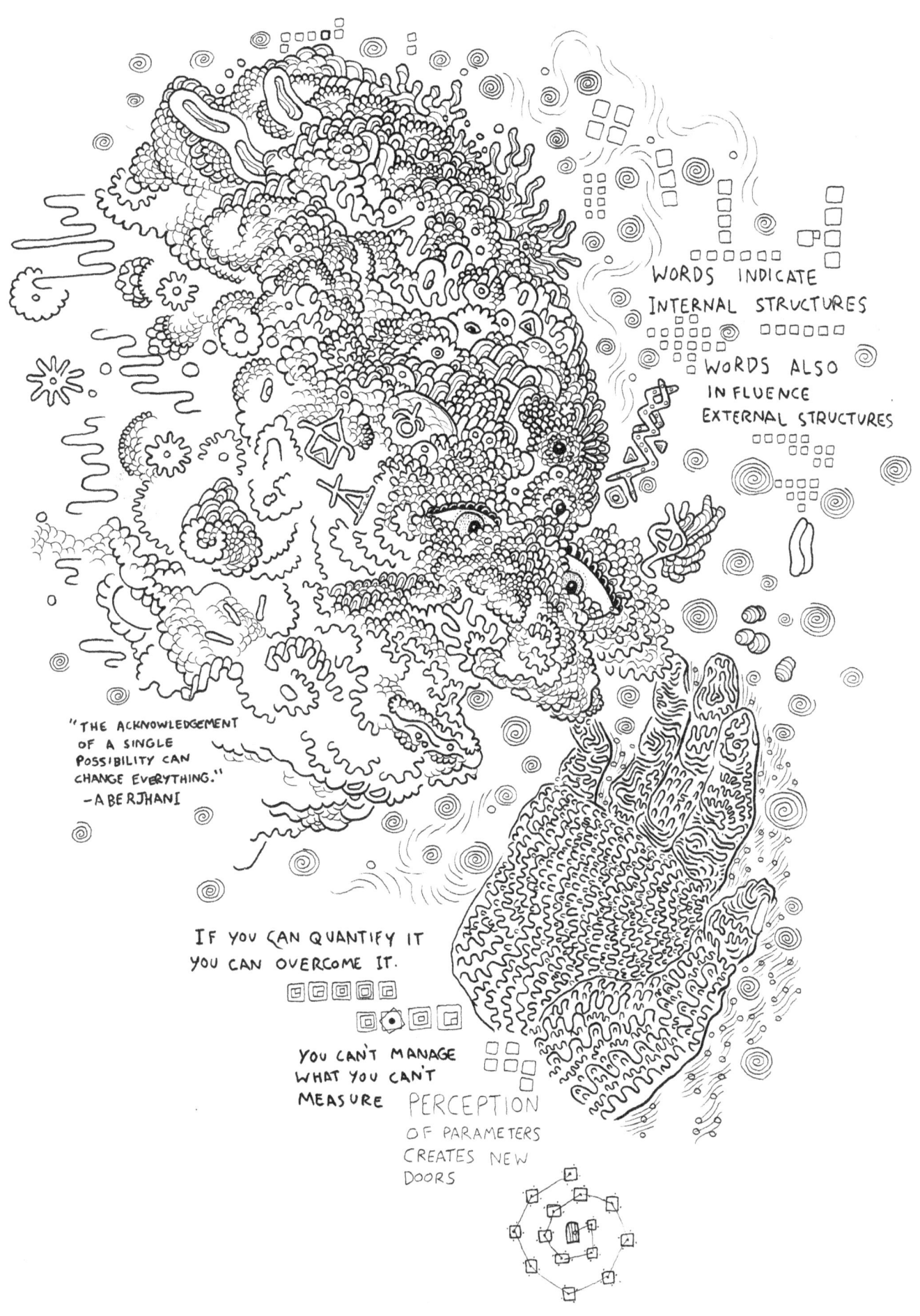

WORDS INDICATE INTERNAL STRUCTURES

WORDS ALSO INFLUENCE EXTERNAL STRUCTURES

"THE ACKNOWLEDGEMENT OF A SINGLE POSSIBILITY CAN CHANGE EVERYTHING."
-ABERJHANI

IF YOU CAN QUANTIFY IT YOU CAN OVERCOME IT.

YOU CAN'T MANAGE WHAT YOU CAN'T MEASURE

PERCEPTION OF PARAMETERS CREATES NEW DOORS

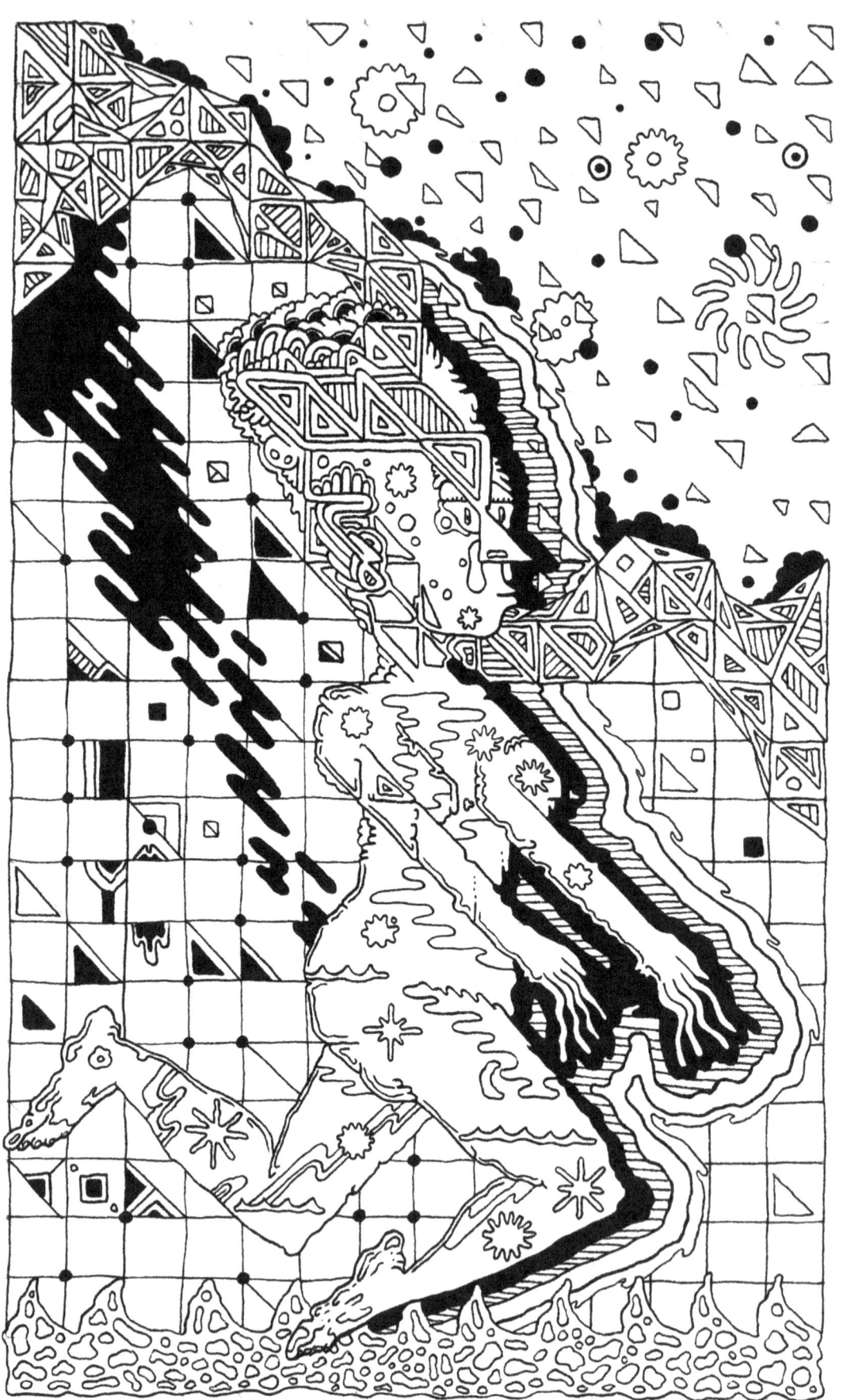

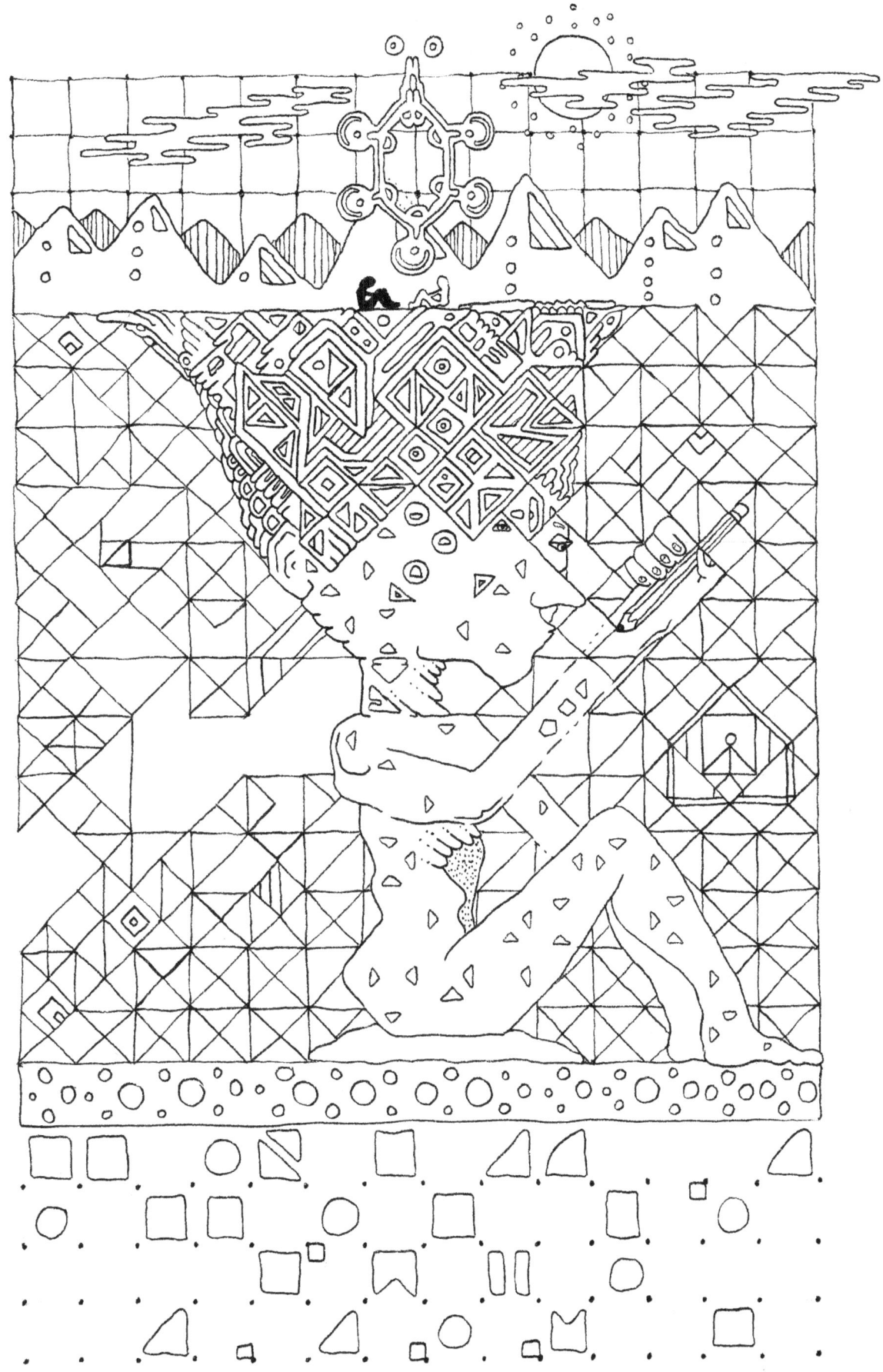

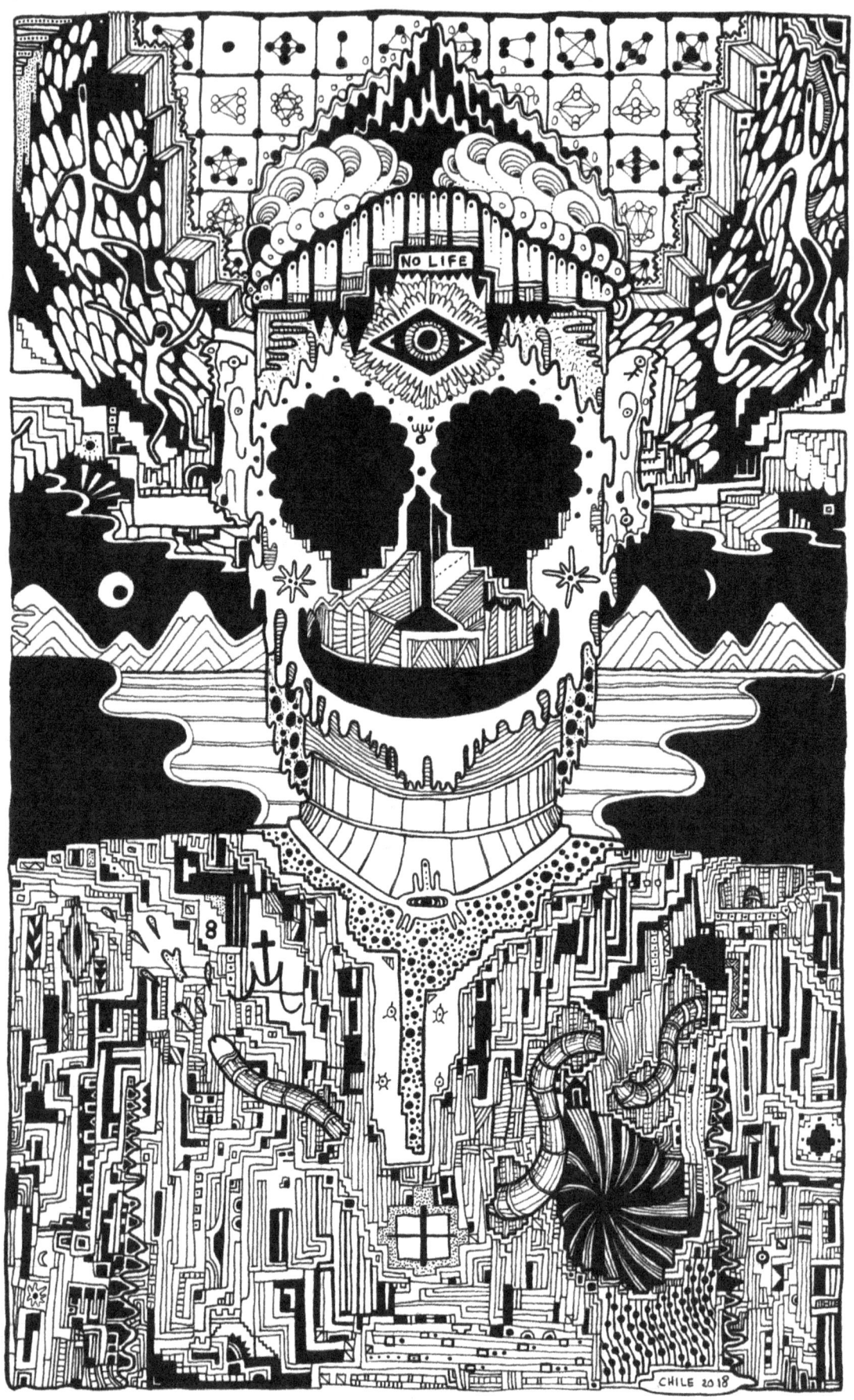

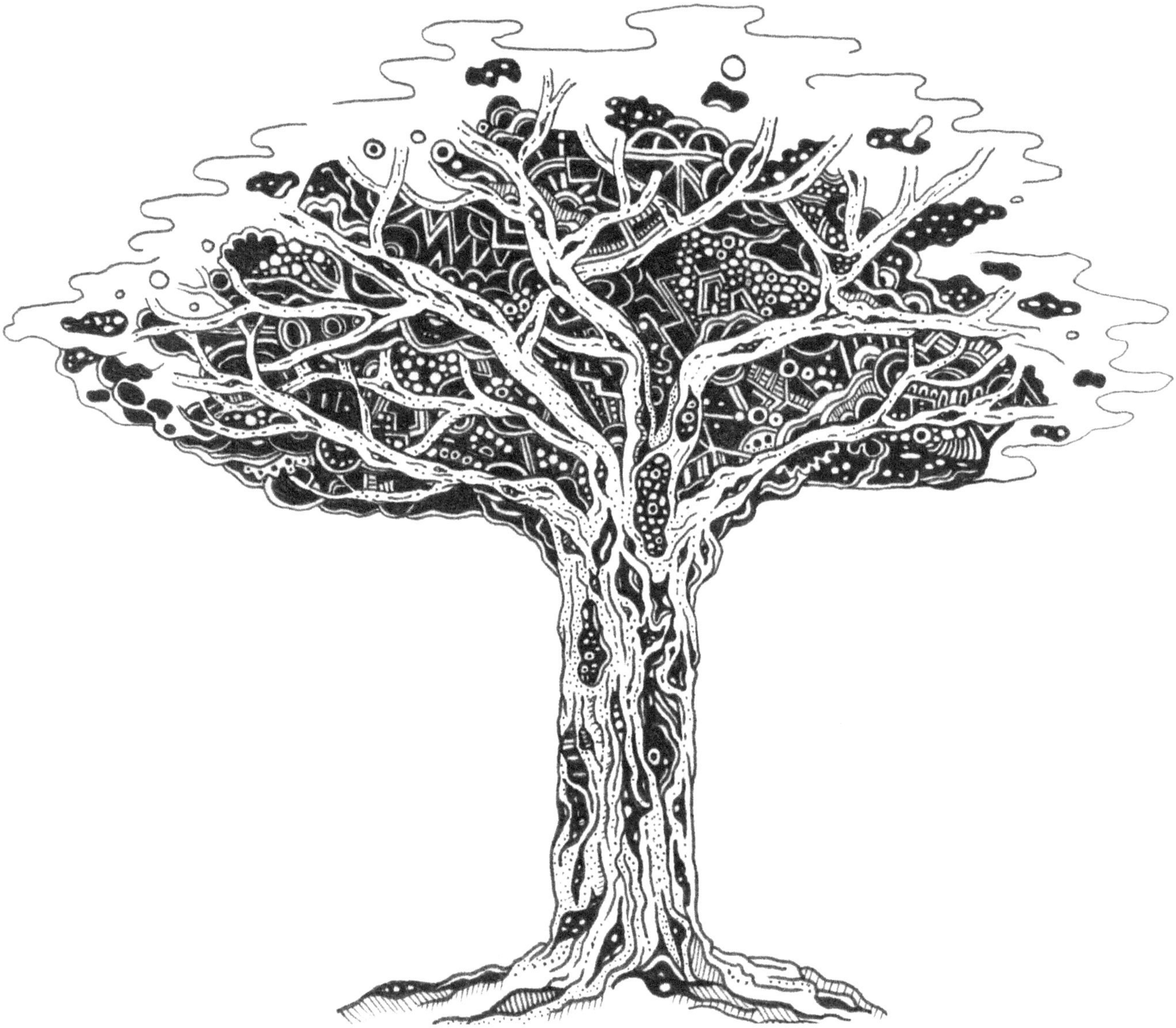

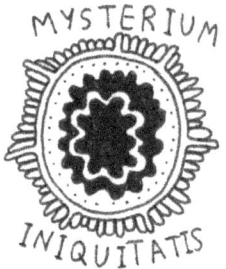

MYSTERIUM

INIQUITATIS

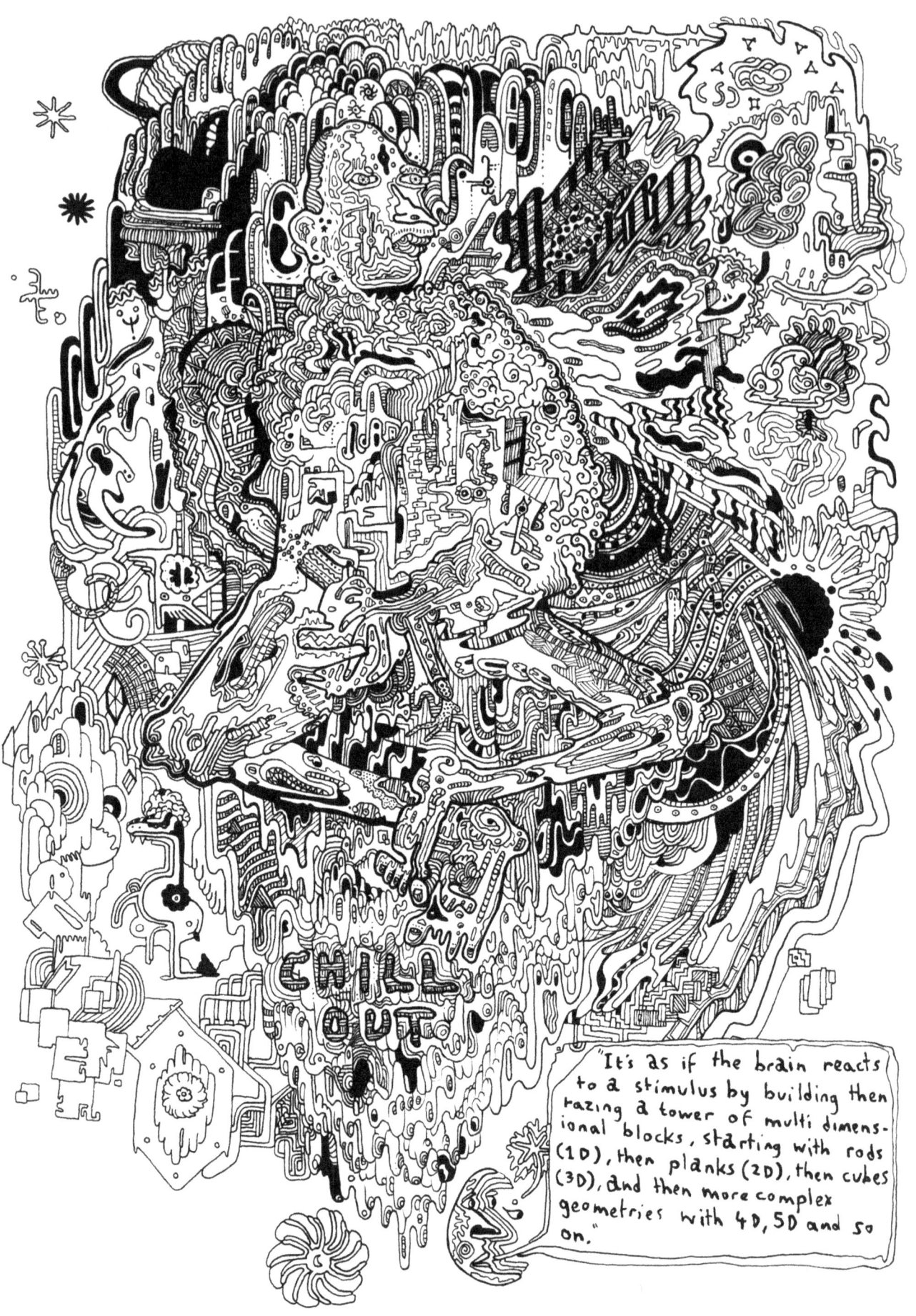

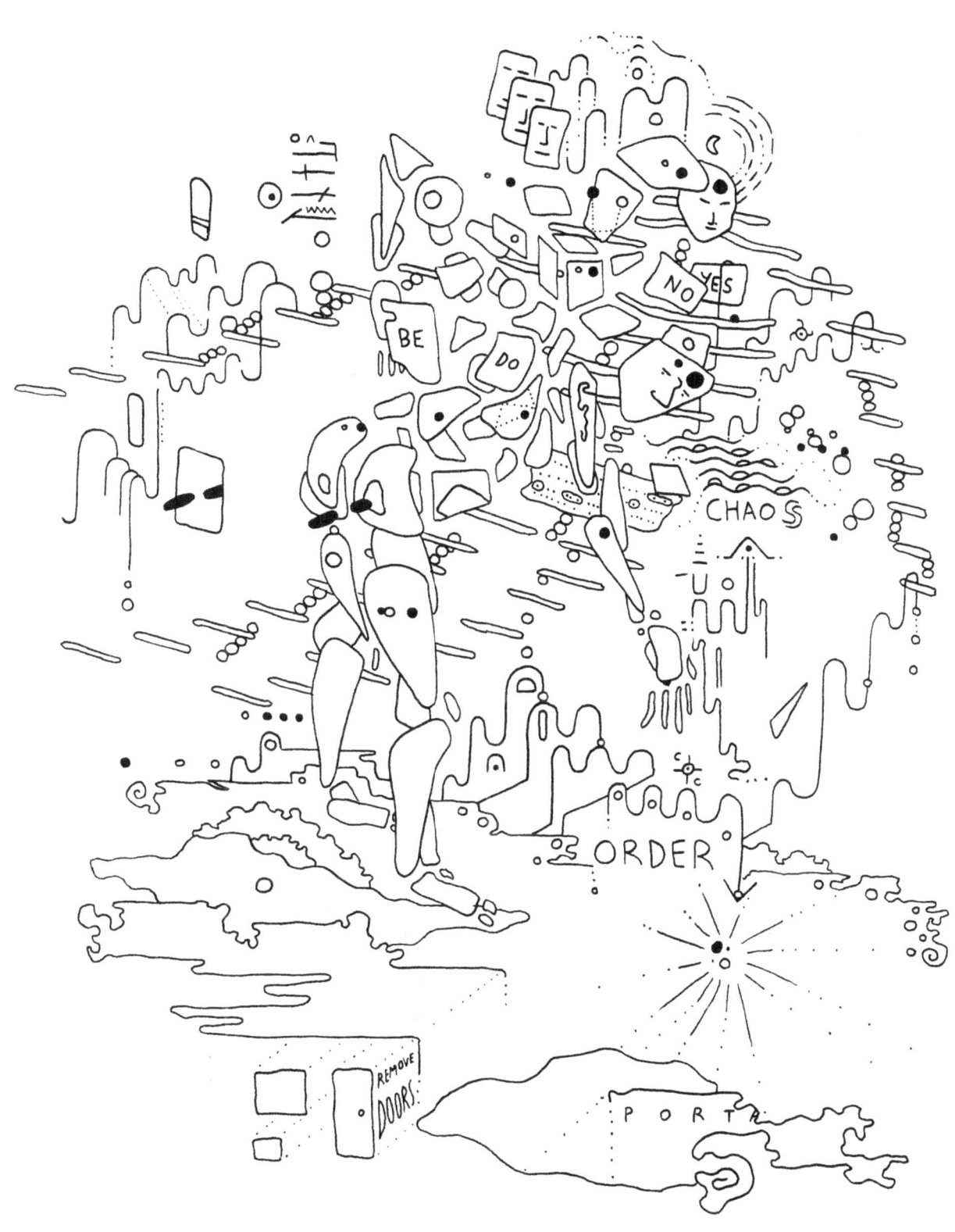

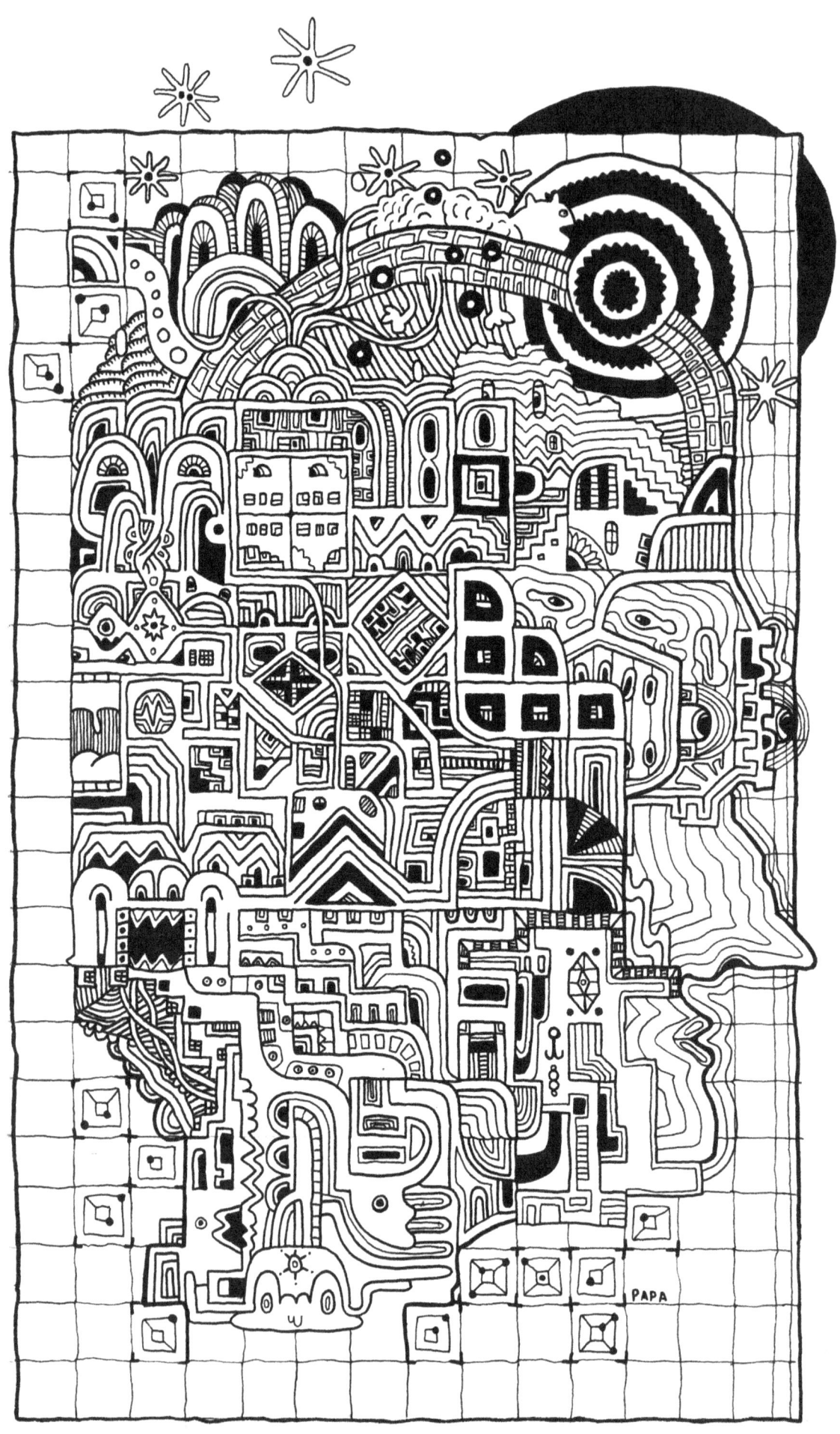

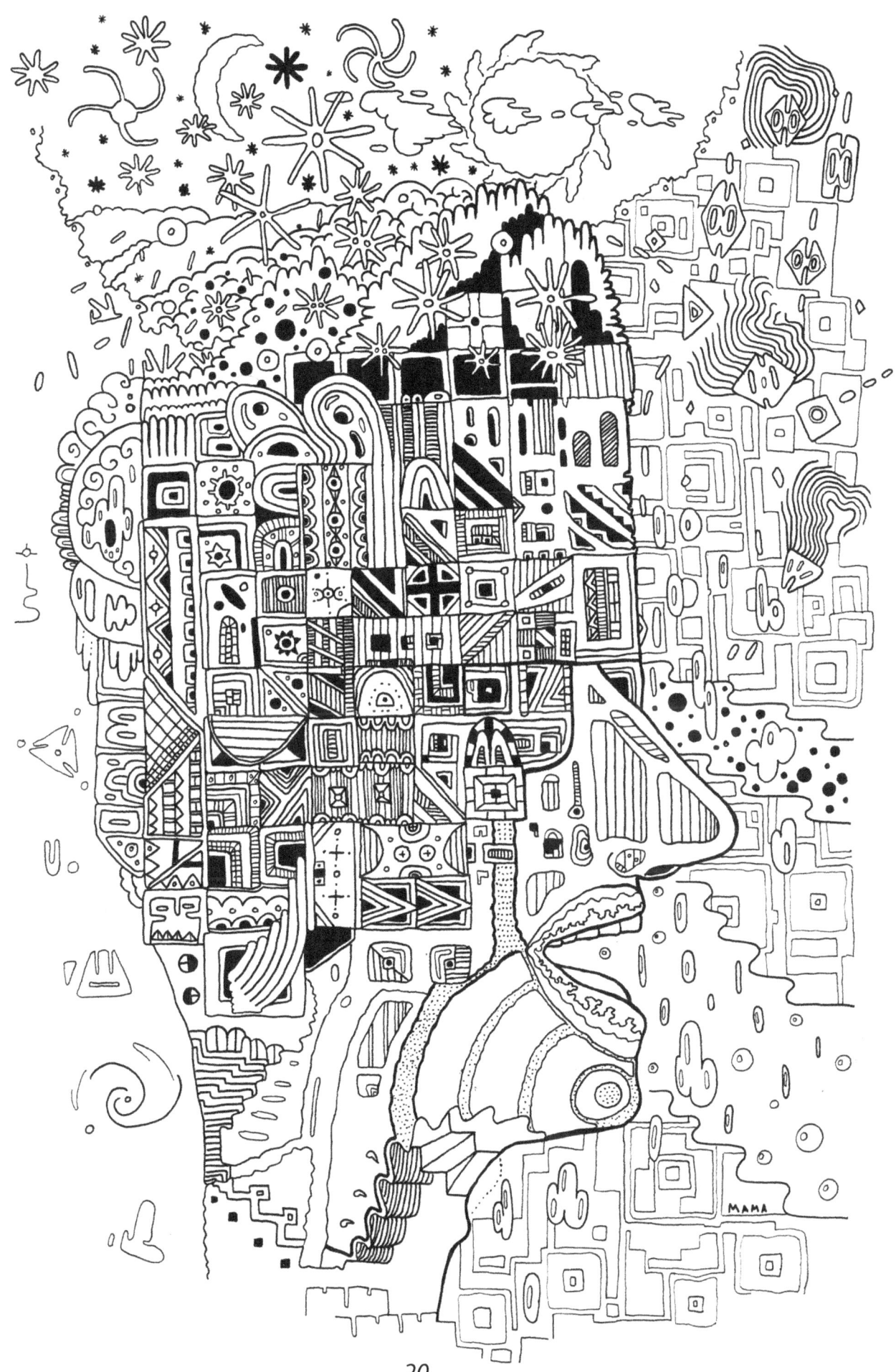

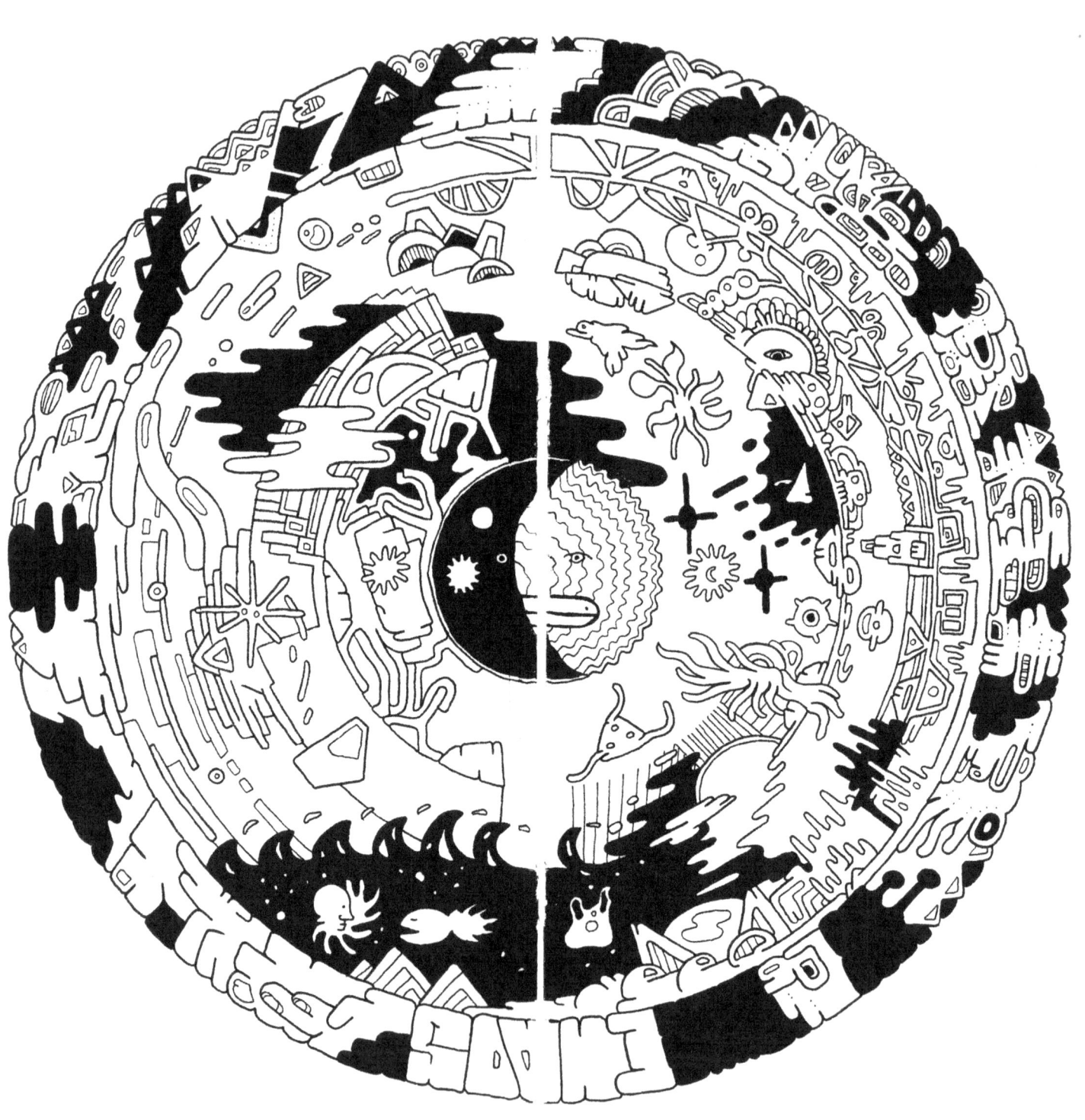

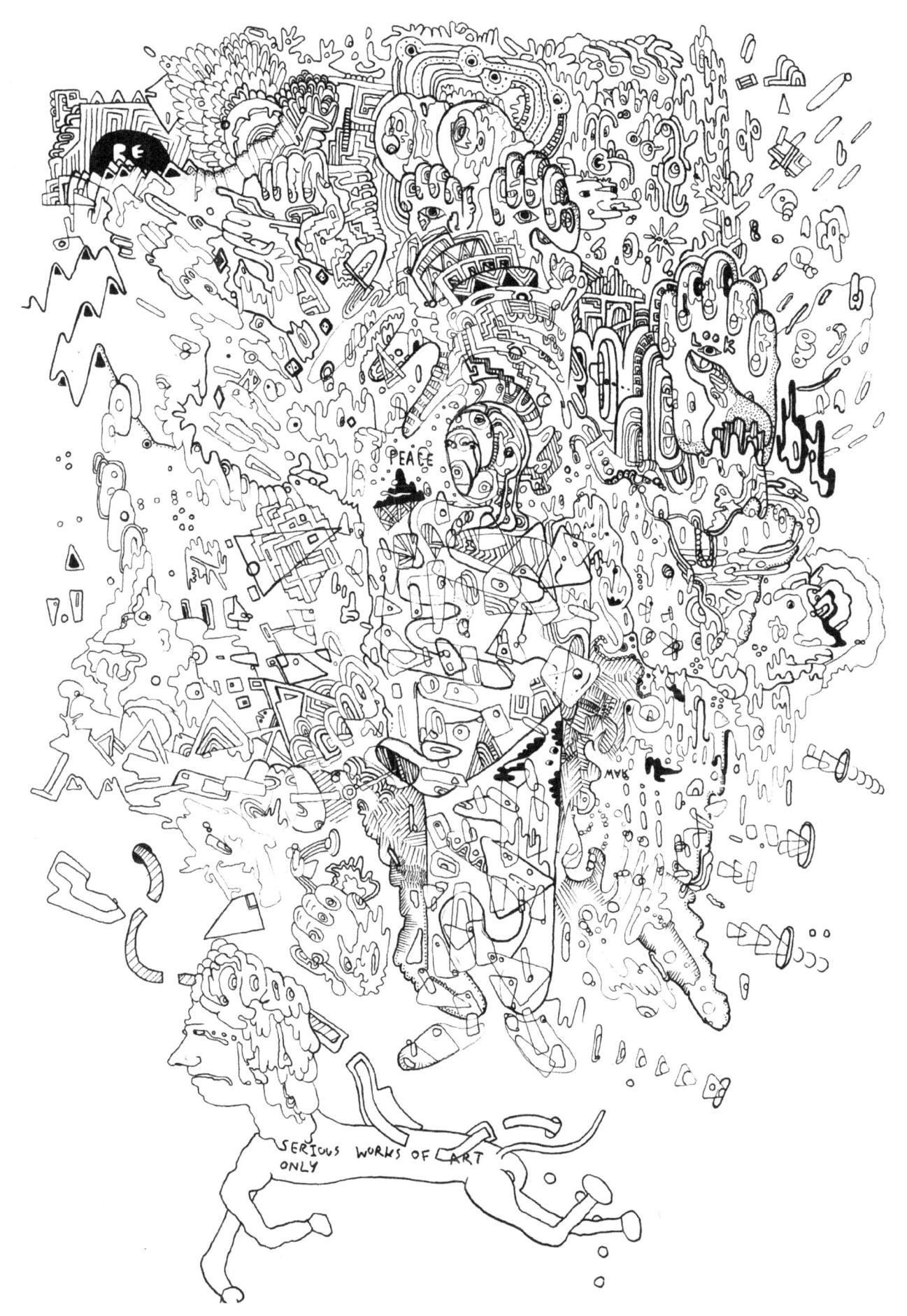

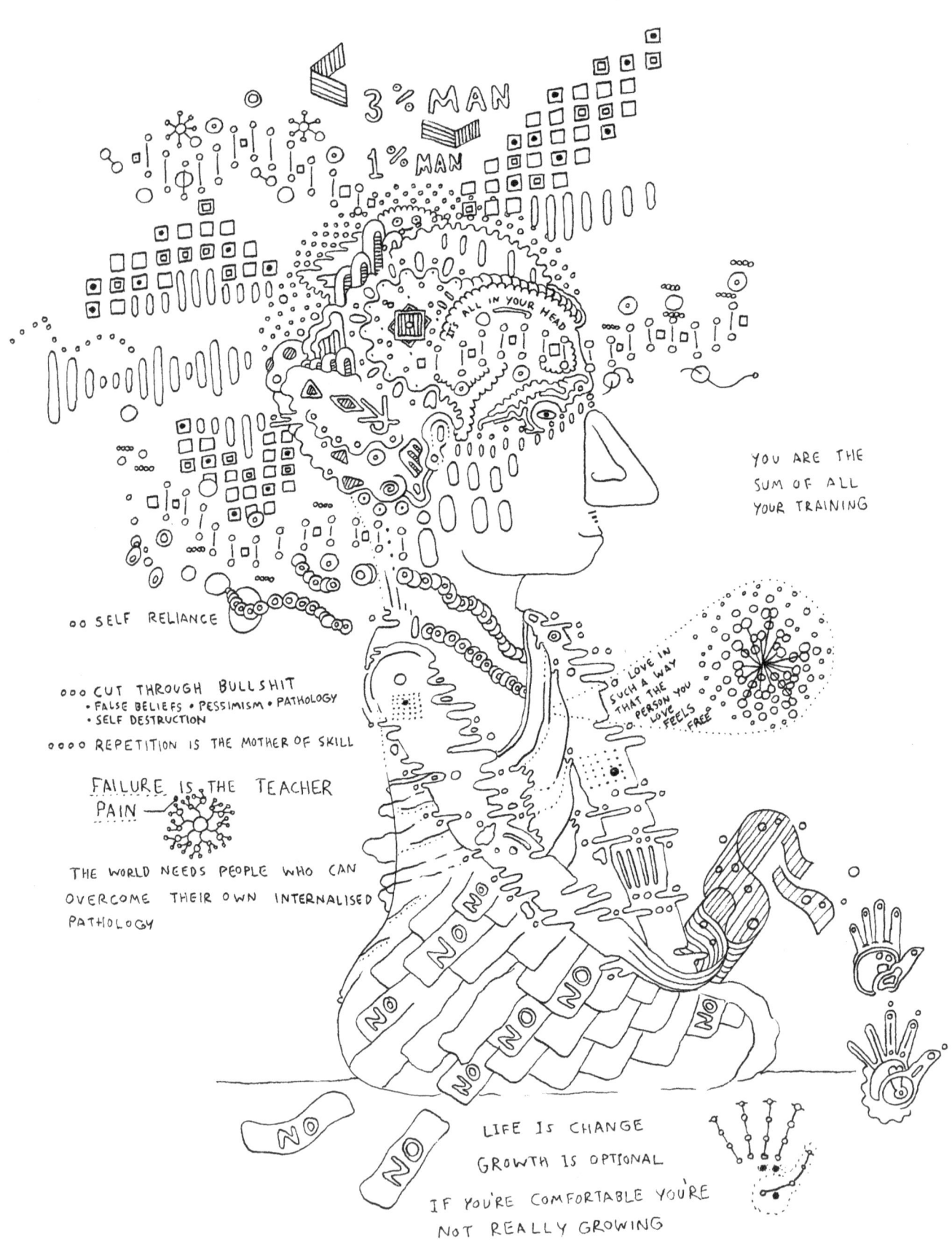

3% MAN

1% MAN

IF ALL IN YOUR HEAD

YOU ARE THE
SUM OF ALL
YOUR TRAINING

oo SELF RELIANCE

ooo CUT THROUGH BULLSHIT
• FALSE BELIEFS • PESSIMISM • PATHOLOGY
• SELF DESTRUCTION

oooo REPETITION IS THE MOTHER OF SKILL

FAILURE IS THE TEACHER
PAIN

THE WORLD NEEDS PEOPLE WHO CAN
OVERCOME THEIR OWN INTERNALISED
PATHOLOGY

LOVE IN
SUCH A WAY
THAT THE
PERSON YOU
LOVE
FEELS
FREE

NO NO NO NO NO NO NO NO NO

LIFE IS CHANGE
GROWTH IS OPTIONAL
IF YOU'RE COMFORTABLE YOU'RE
NOT REALLY GROWING

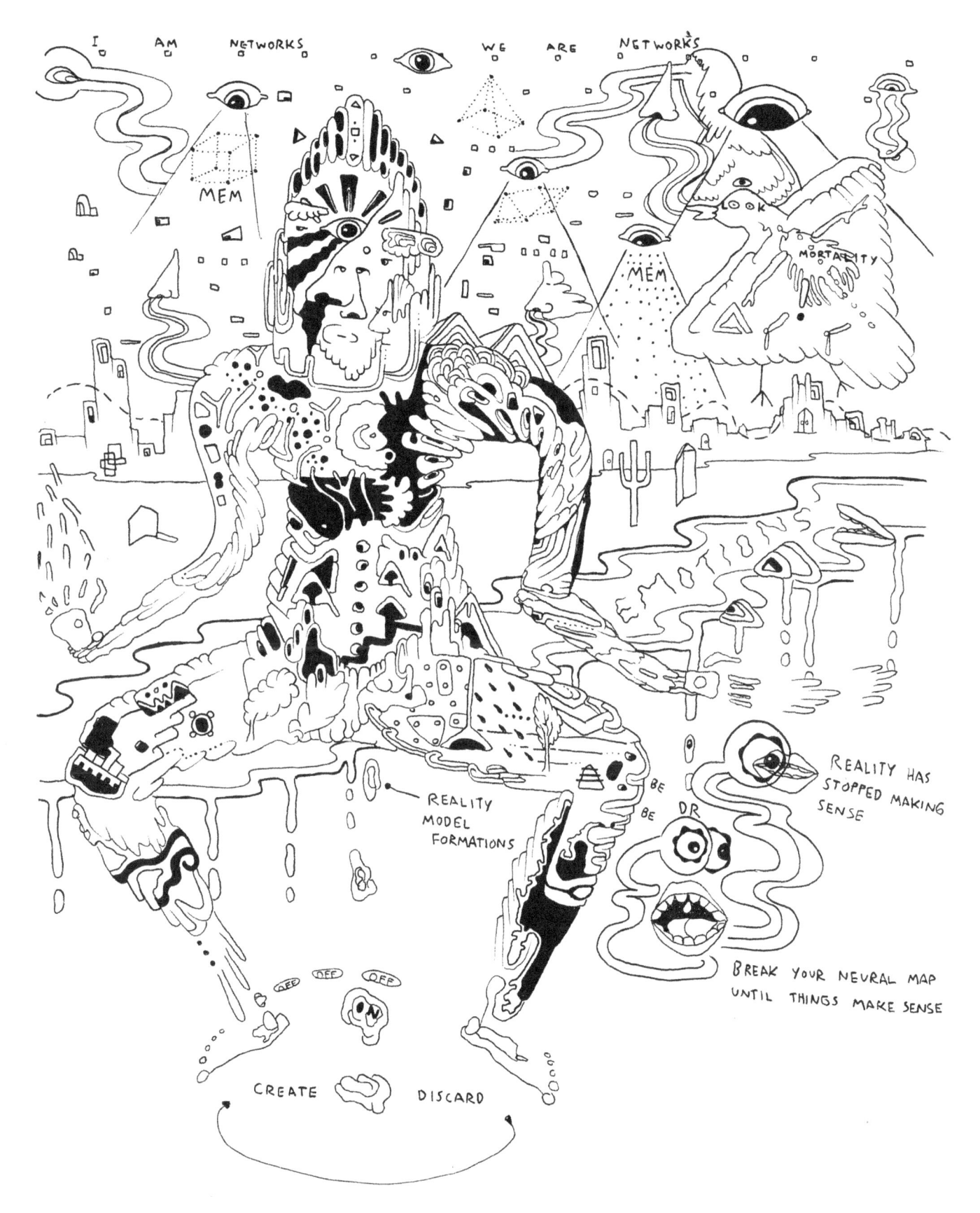

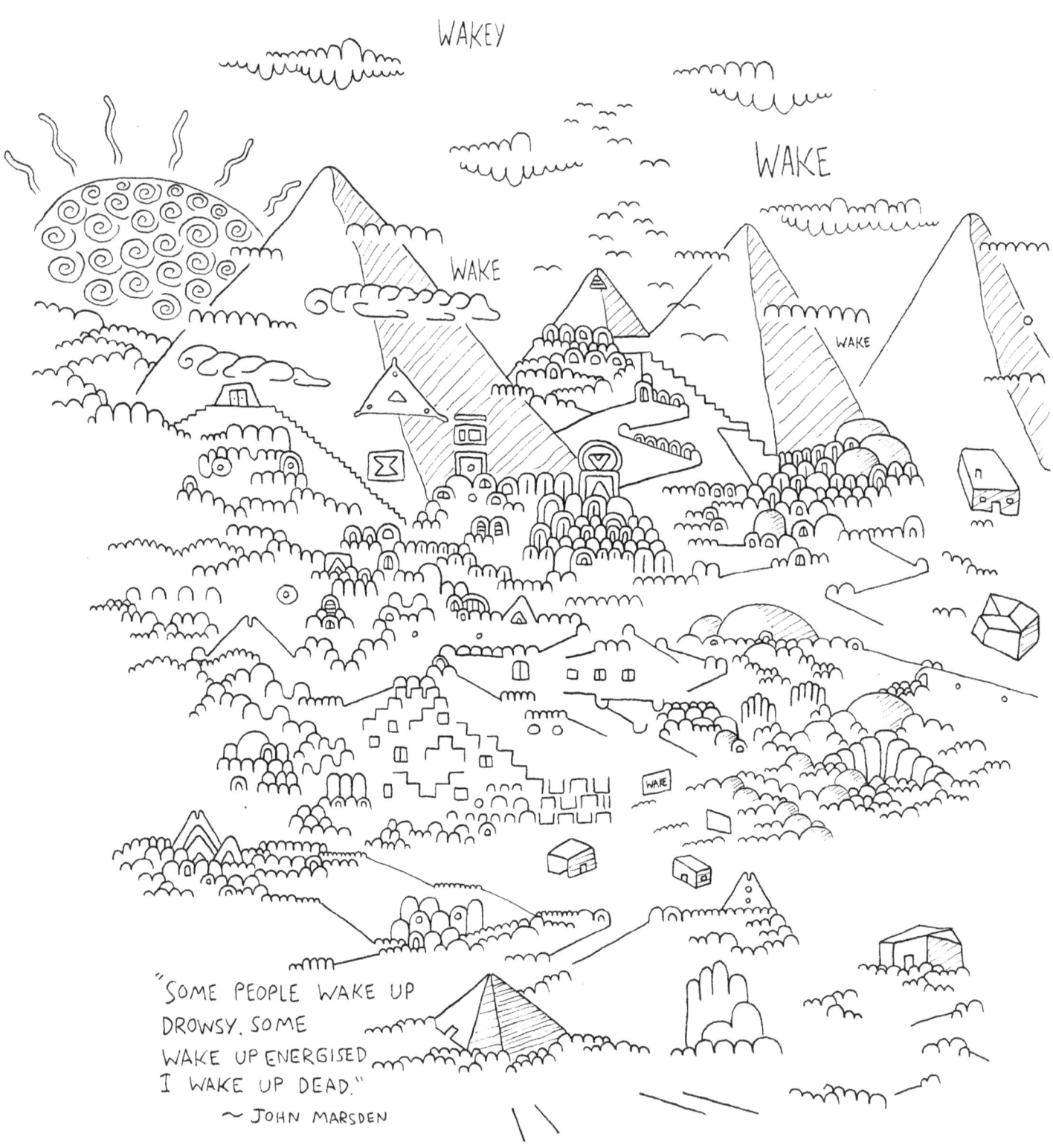

"SOME PEOPLE WAKE UP
DROWSY. SOME
WAKE UP ENERGISED.
I WAKE UP DEAD."
~ JOHN MARSDEN

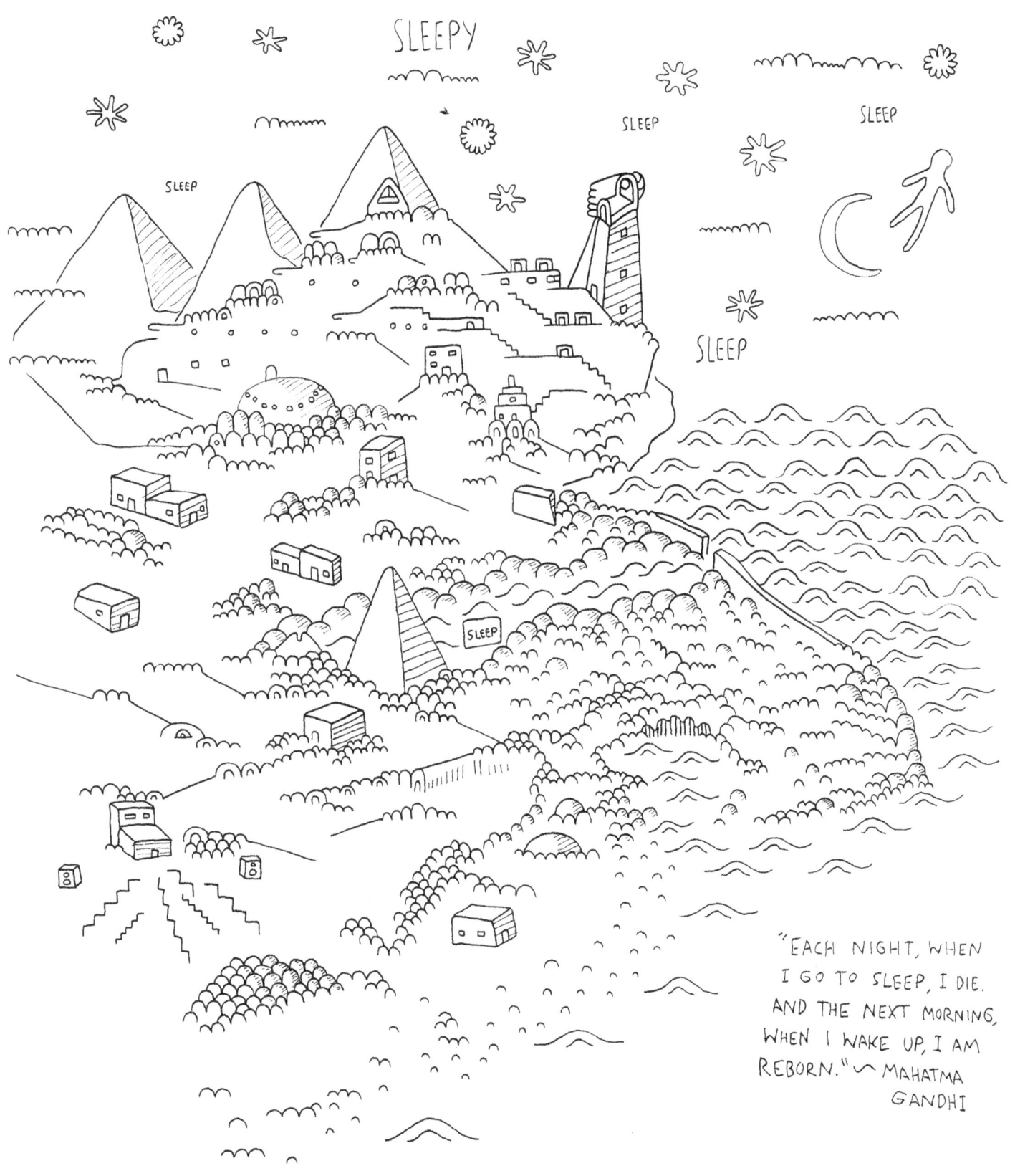

SLEEPY

SLEEP

SLEEP

SLEEP

SLEEP

SLEEP

"EACH NIGHT, WHEN I GO TO SLEEP, I DIE. AND THE NEXT MORNING, WHEN I WAKE UP, I AM REBORN." — MAHATMA GANDHI

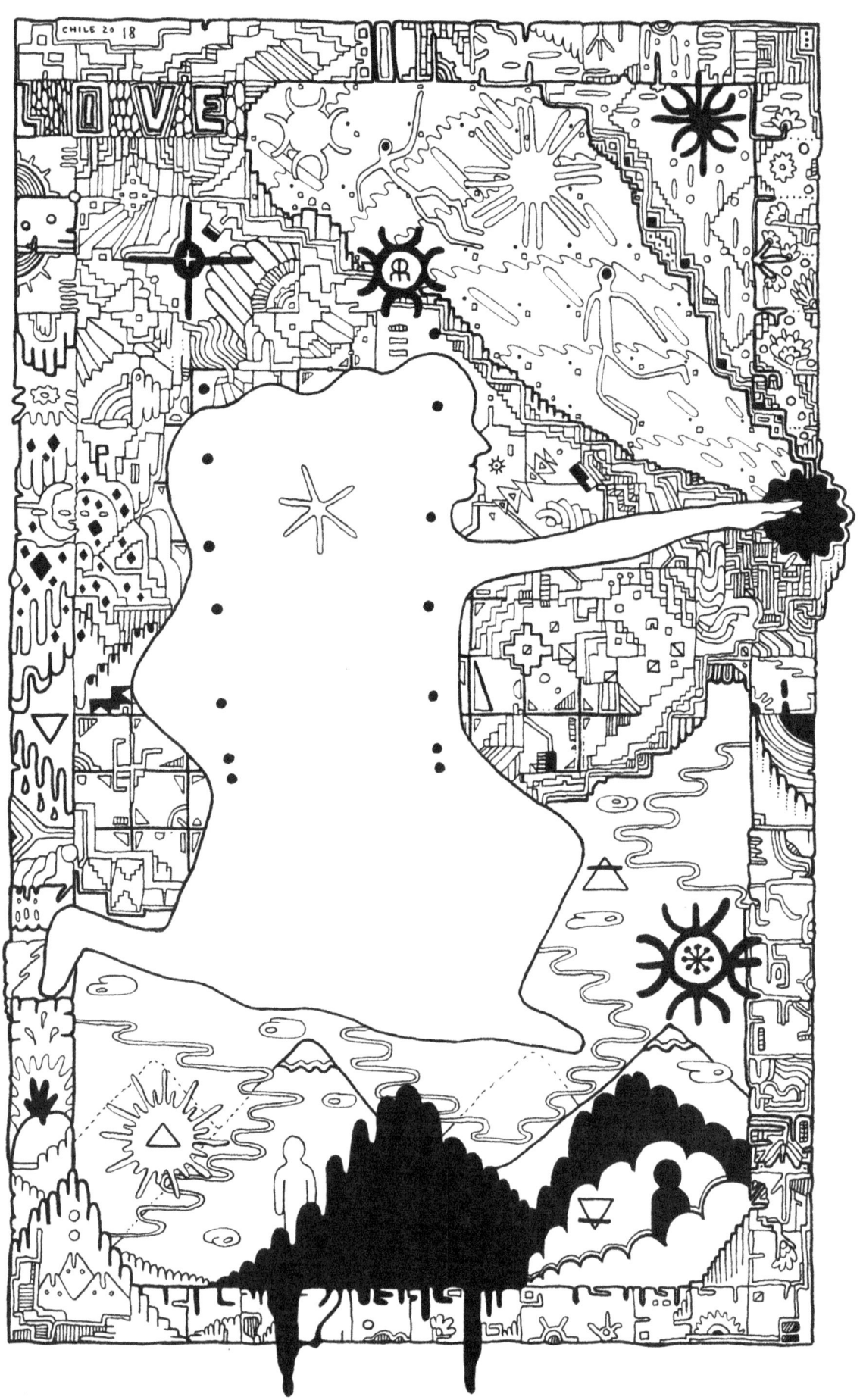

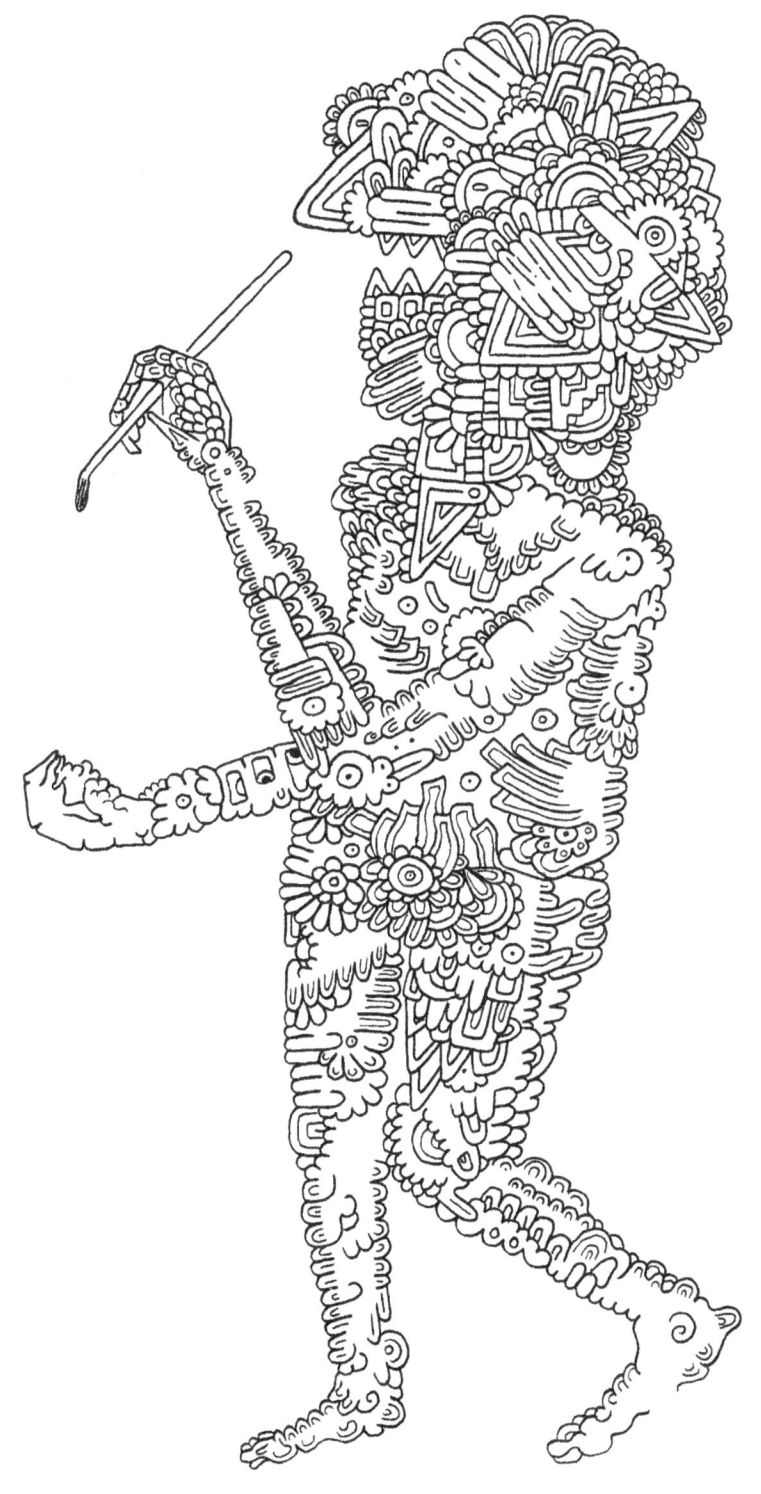

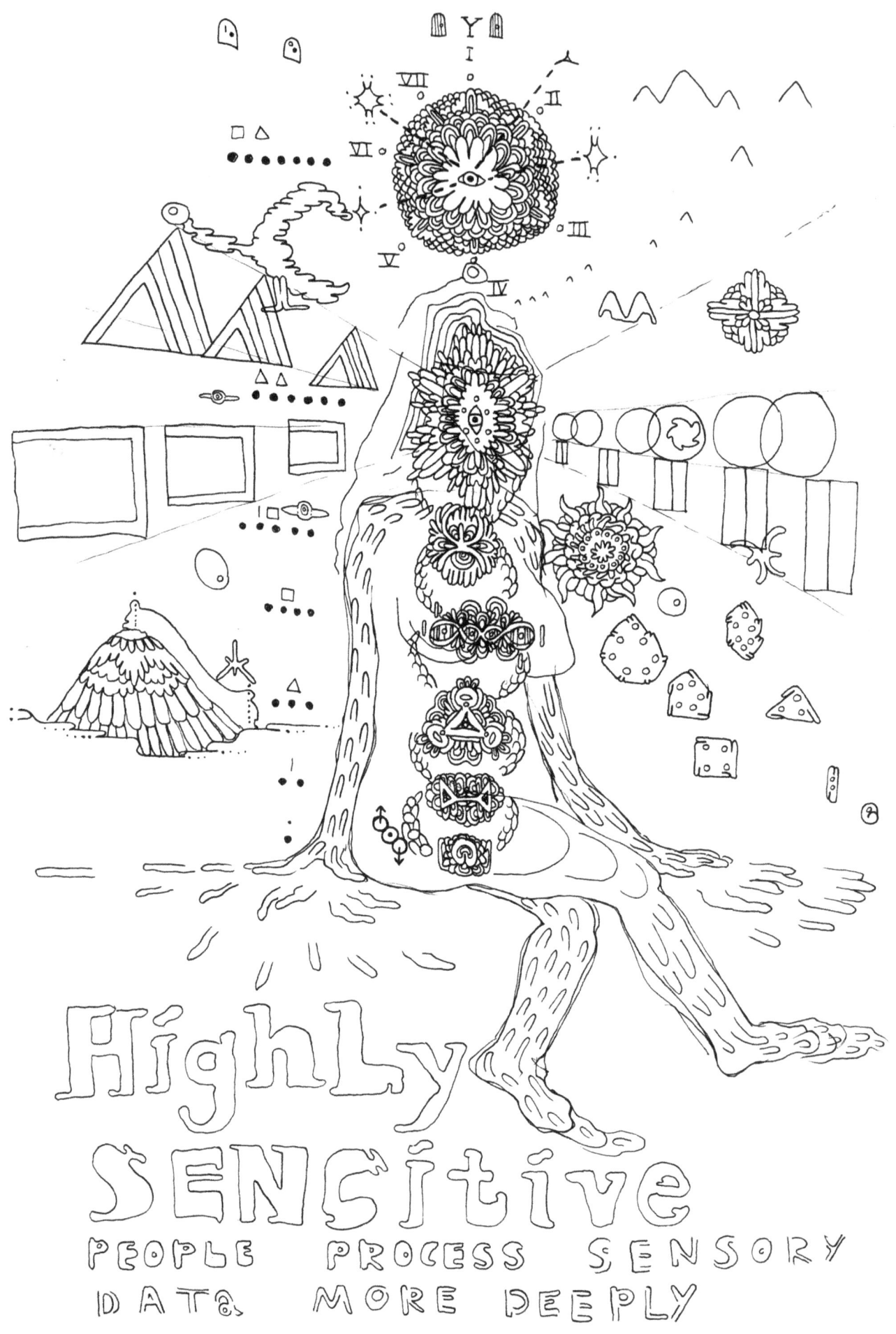

Highly Sensitive

PEOPLE PROCESS SENSORY
DATA MORE DEEPLY

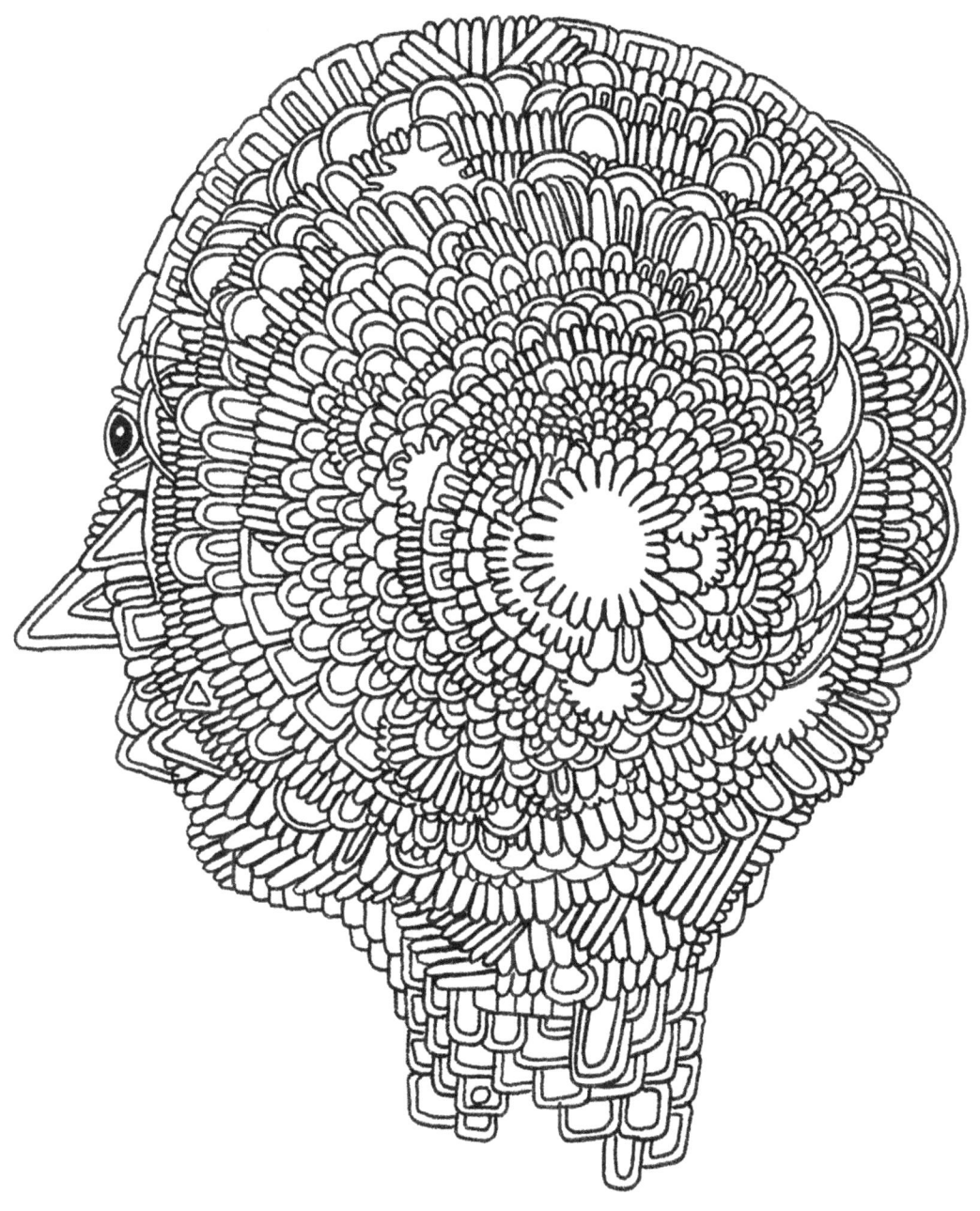

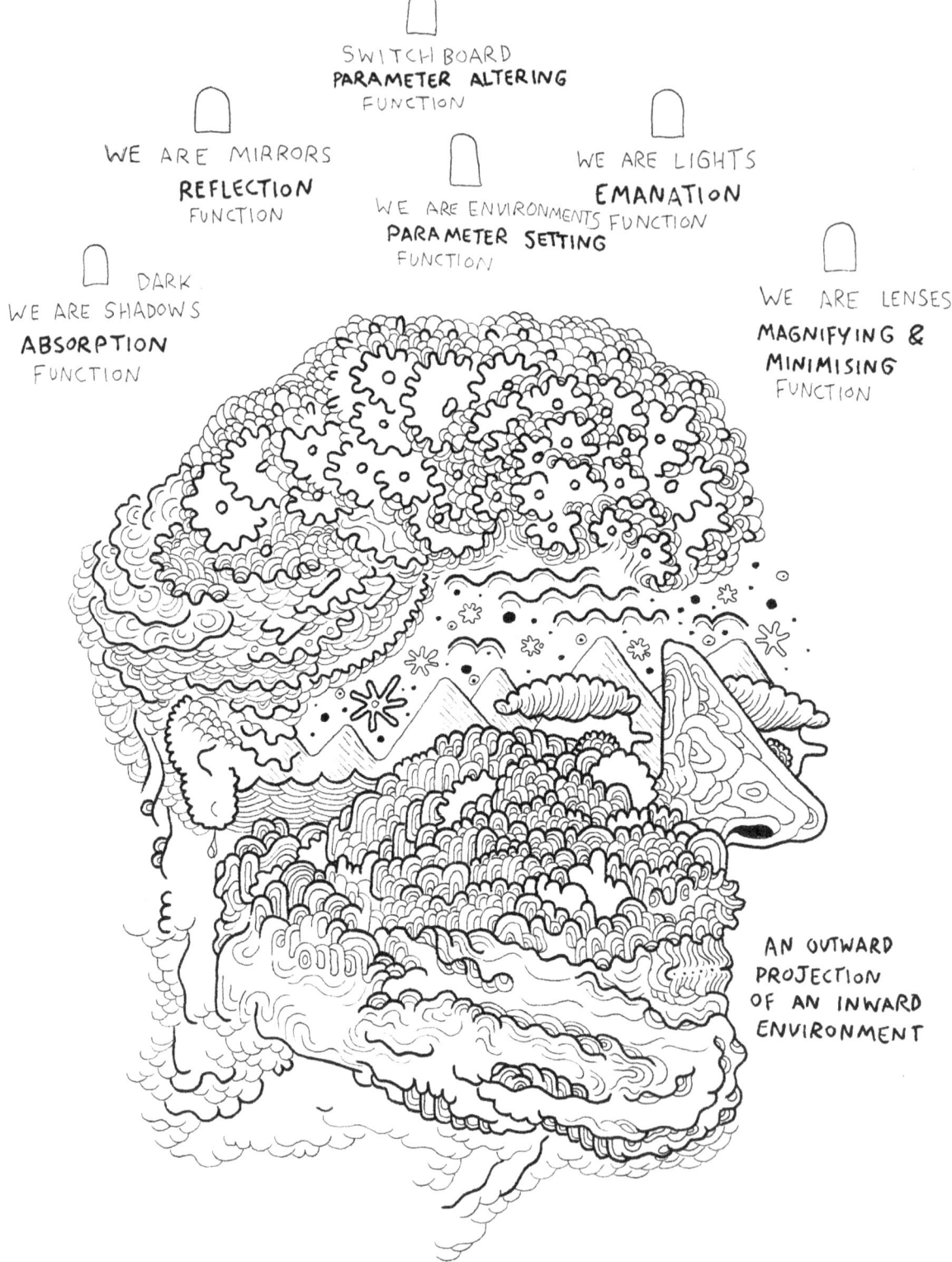

SWITCH BOARD
PARAMETER ALTERING
FUNCTION

WE ARE MIRRORS
REFLECTION
FUNCTION

WE ARE LIGHTS
EMANATION
FUNCTION

WE ARE ENVIRONMENTS
PARAMETER SETTING
FUNCTION

DARK
WE ARE SHADOWS
ABSORPTION
FUNCTION

WE ARE LENSES
**MAGNIFYING &
MINIMISING**
FUNCTION

AN OUTWARD
PROJECTION
OF AN INWARD
ENVIRONMENT

"I WAS WALKING AMONG THE FIRES OF HELL,
DELIGHTED WITH THE ENJOYMENTS OF GENIUS;
WHICH TO ANGELS LOOK LIKE TORMENT & INSANITY."

~ WILLIAM BLAKE

GENIUS AS A FORM OF PSYCHIC MASOCHISM — NO MUD, NO LOTUS

31

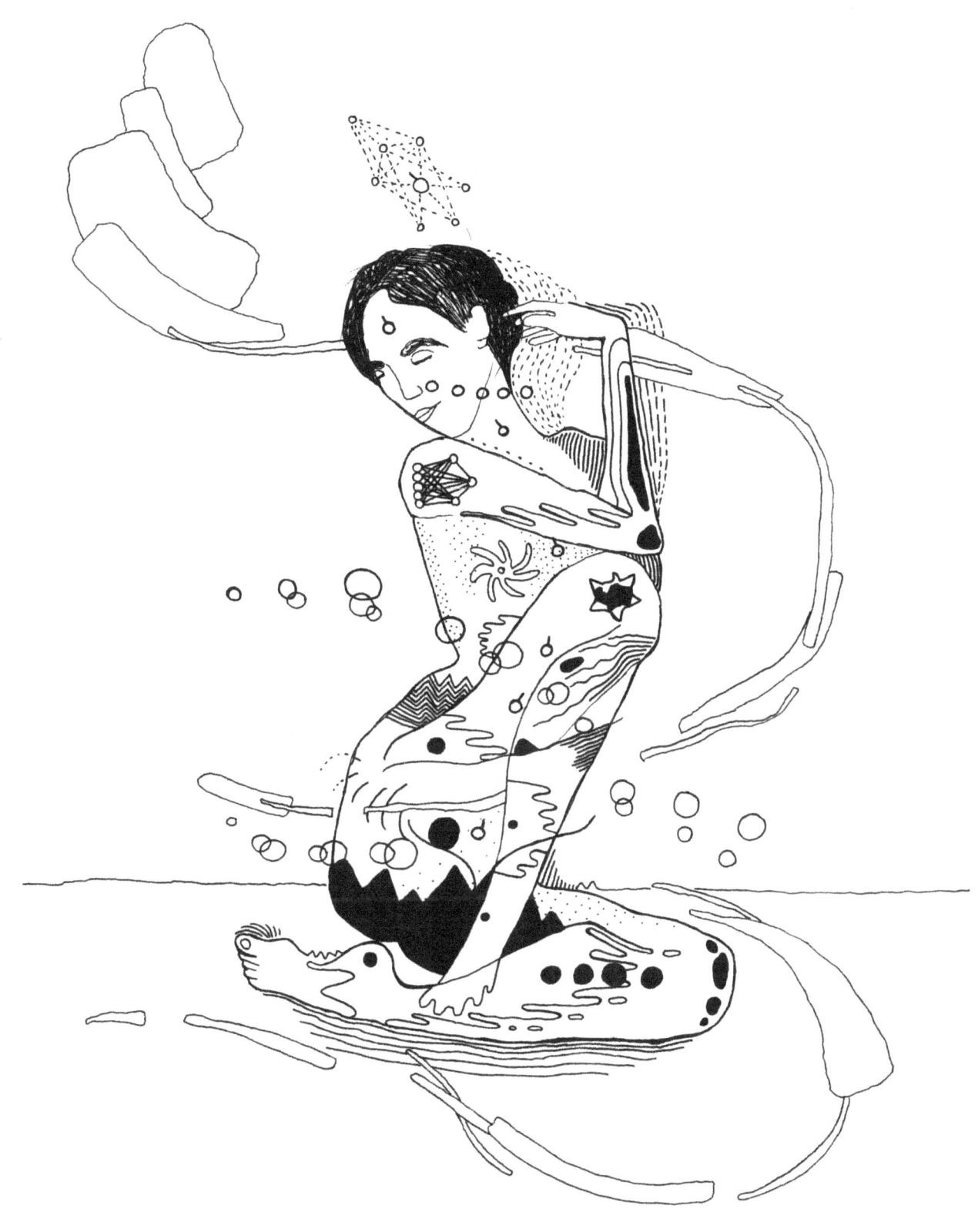

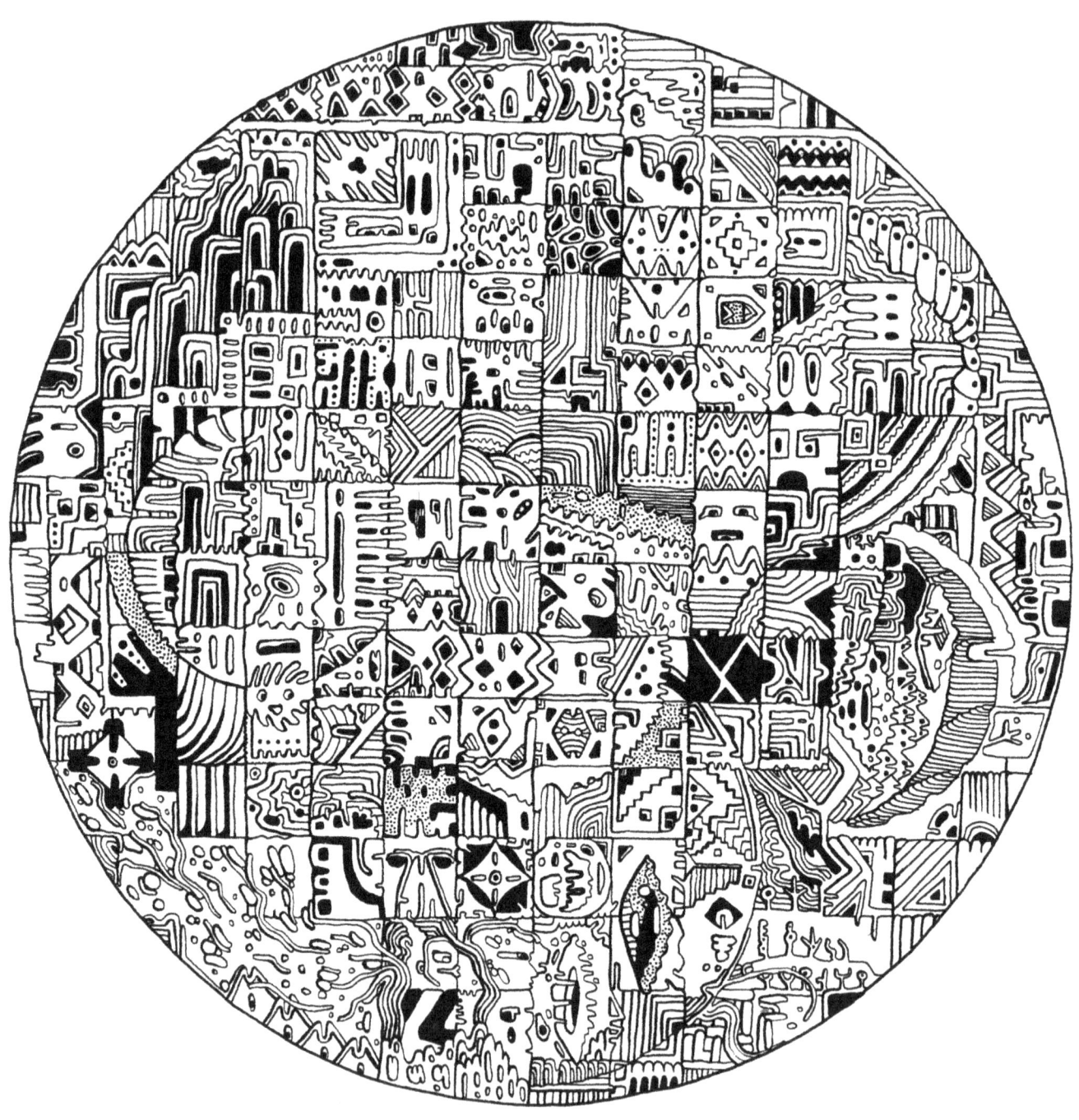

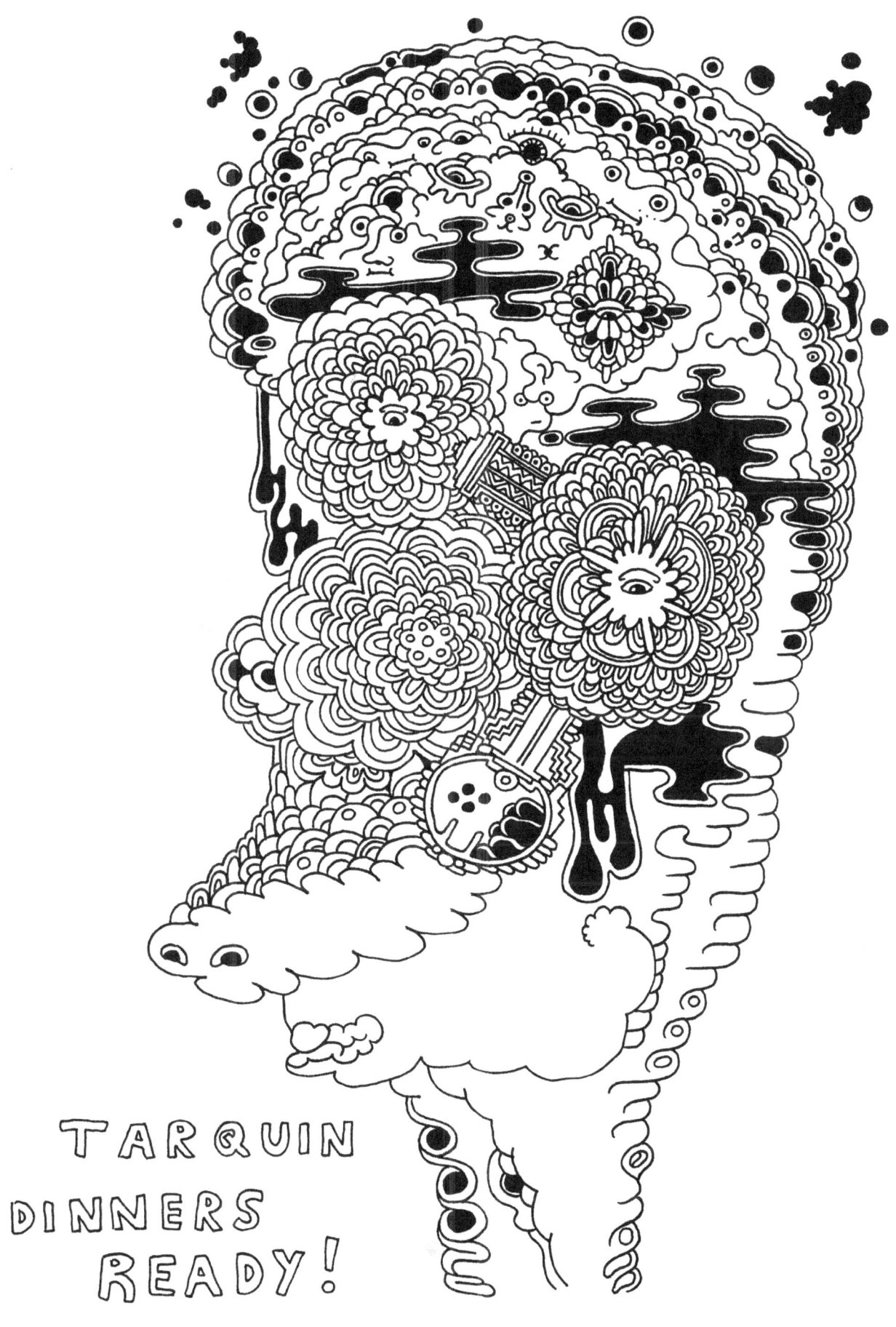

TARQUIN
DINNERS
READY!

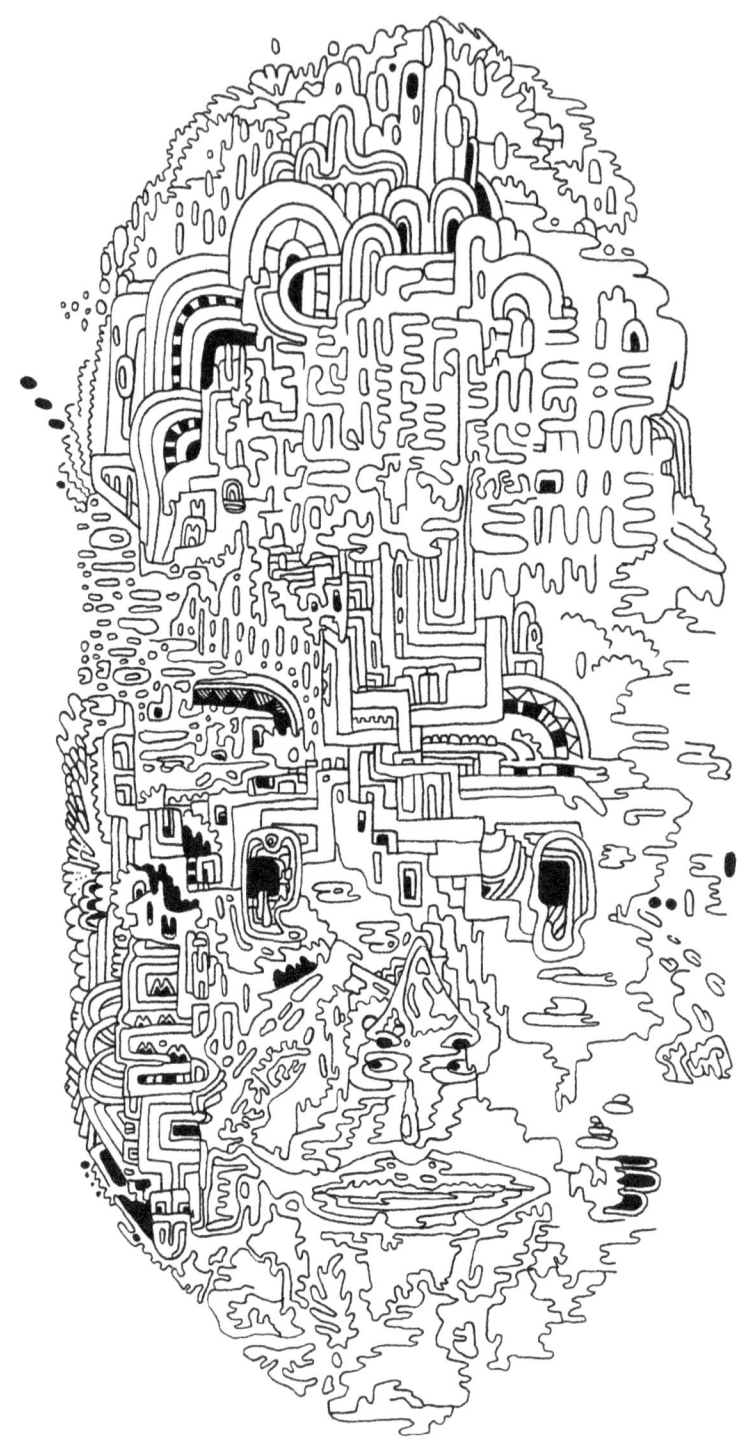

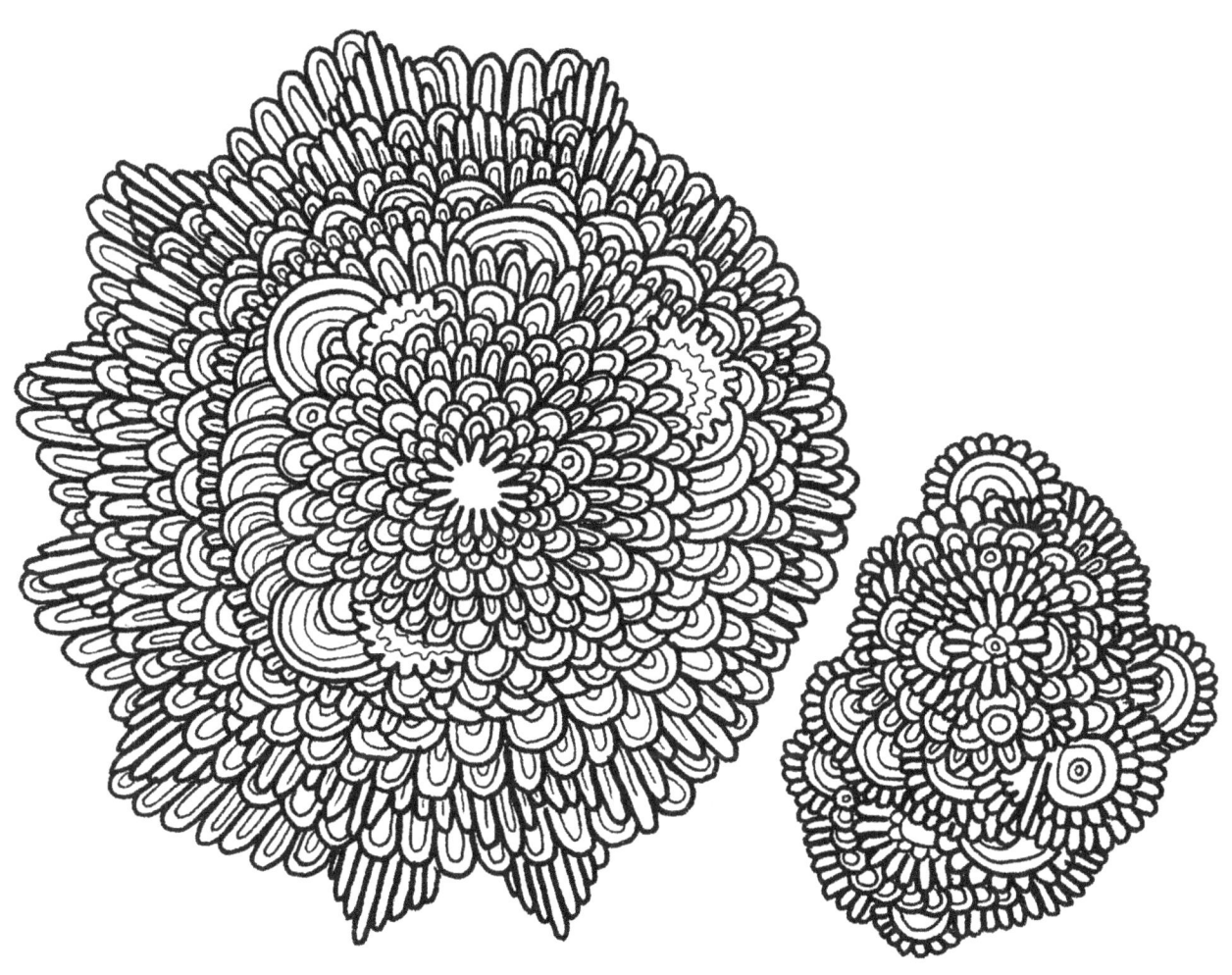

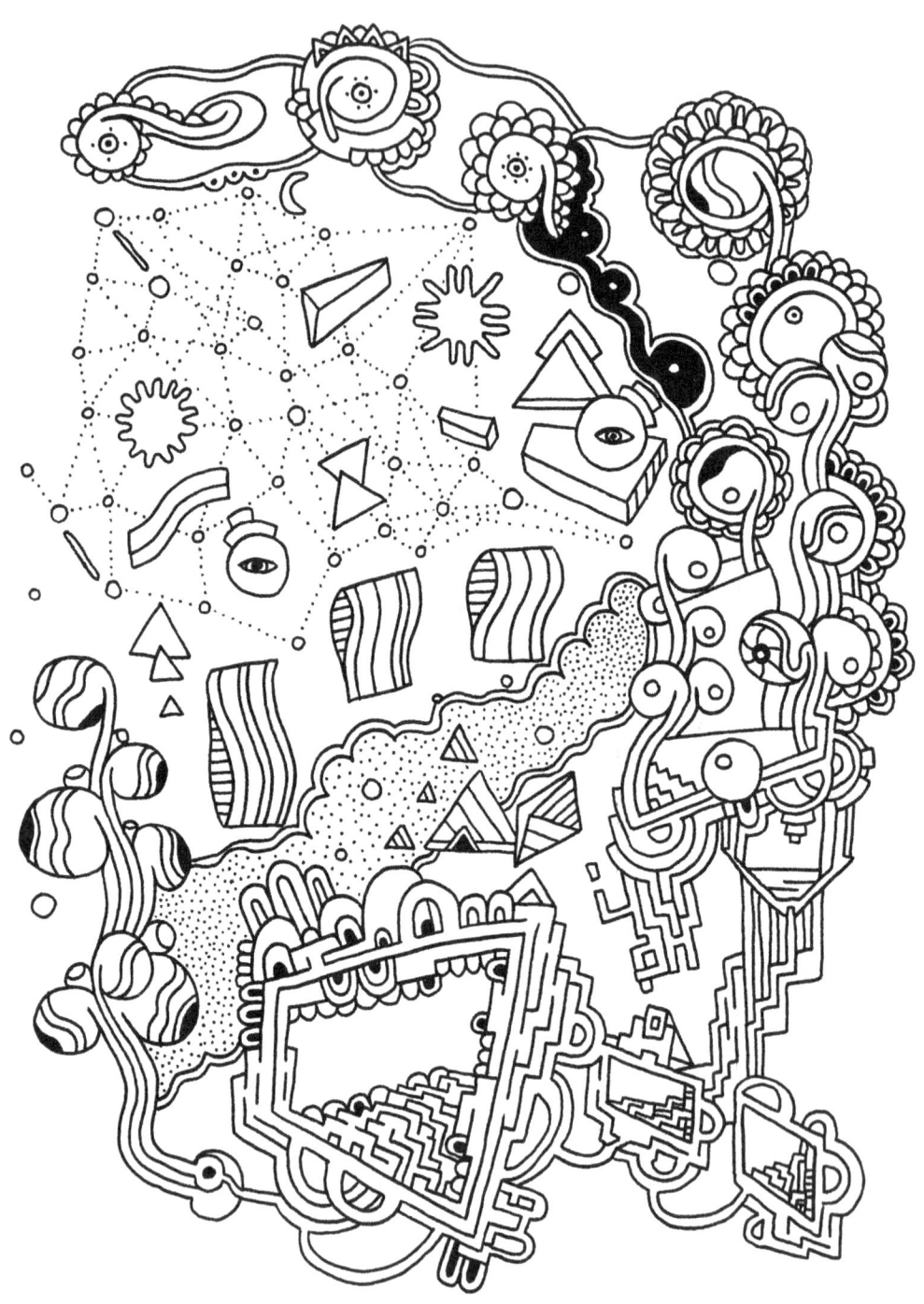

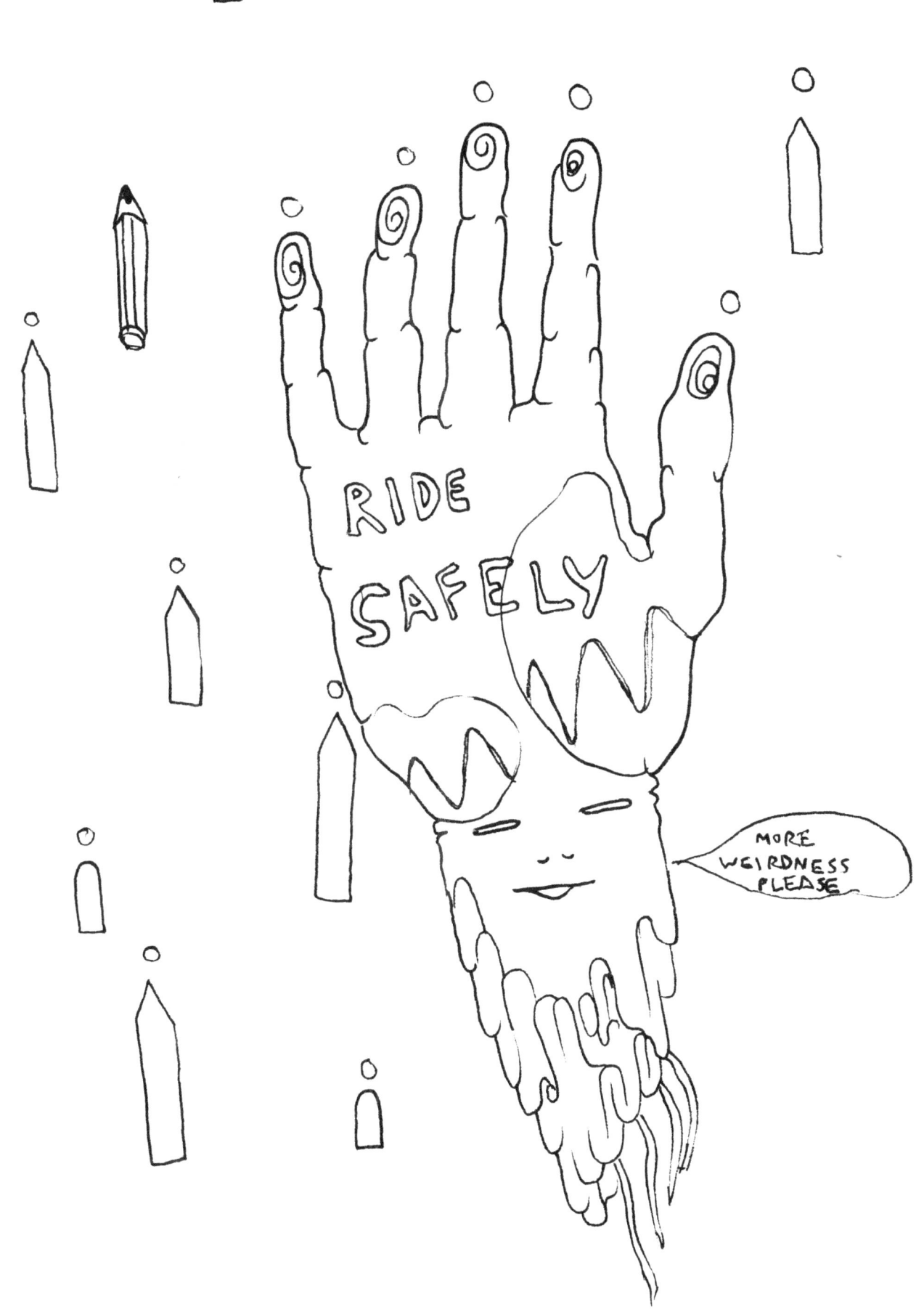